CHOOSE PEACE

"Rina is simply a wonderful coach. She's young, beautiful, intelligent, driven, kind, spiritual, deep and fun! She has a very special gift for communication. She can explain something that can literally change your life in a very relaxed and practical way. I believe that in the next years, Rina will be touching the lives of hundreds of thousands of people through mass media and using the yoga practice as a tool that can be used by anyone at anytime to live a better life".

— **Marco Antonio Regil, TV Host/ Producer**

"With the skills of a wise teacher and the voice of a best friend, Rina Jakubowicz gently guides her readers along the path to inner peace. Skillfully weaving in experiences from her own life and from yoga teachings, the author reveals ancient truths about mindfulness, nonjudgment, compassion, and the workings of the ego using examples and practical steps to which any modern reader will relate. This book doesn't merely instruct us to choose peace; it shows us exactly how to overcome the negative thoughts and behaviors that stand in its way."

- **Amy Weiss, MSW**

"Rina is a powerful yogini."

— **Mark Whitwell, Renowned Yoga Teacher**

"The 15 Steps are a brilliant idea to get straight to the point of what is disturbing your inner peace. I have read quite a few books about self awareness and this is so far the one that has best worked for me....I love it! "

- **Brenda Delgado, Yoga Student**

"I went to Rina's book signing/discussion the day before one of the biggest auditions of my career thus far. She explained the roles of the big Self and the little self (the ego) and how they affect our peace. By the time I read with producers (including the star of the show) I could have been my usual mess but instead I owned my power and while I made eye contact with all 10 heads in the room I repeated (in my head of course!) "they are all atoms" and the nerves turned into excitement and kick-ass-ness! I shined through the audition and garnered laughs from many of them, mostly the star/producer. I left the room on cloud nine and I will always remember this day as the best audition I've delivered yet. All with just a little alignment in my perception thanks to Rina's inspiring words. "

- Krizia Bajos, Actress

"Choose Peace was beautiful. A sweet combination of personal and universal truths, in clear language that would be accessible to anyone, and especially those looking for guidance as they navigate difficult times in their lives."

- Peter Sterios, Master Yoga Teacher and Founder of Manduka

"Choose Peace starts like a thriller and maintains the same momentum until the end. Much of this has to do with a great deal of honesty by the author and simple, concise language that is very easy to understand and goes to the core of the matter. The author proposes one practical suggestion after another to very common challenges we all face. It is an impressive achievement, in my view. This is an excellent book, which should really be up there on the best-seller list in Amazon."

-Dr. Tamay Ozgokmen, Professor, University of Miami

Rina Jakubowicz's

CHOOSE PEACE

A Practical Guide into Consciousness

Second Edition
Just Be Publications
Miami, Florida

RINA JAKUBOWICZ'S CHOOSE PEACE
A Practical Guide into Consciousness
by Rina Jakubowicz
Just Be Publications
3 Gove Isle Dr.   #09
Miami, FL 33133, USA.
www.rinayoga.com

Edition ISBN
Softcover 978-0-615-34293-1

First Edition 2010, Second Edition 2012
Printed in the United States of America.

For Purusha

Thank you for your love, wisdom, and inspiration.

Table of Contents

Rina Jakubowicz, founder of Rina Yoga, is an international bilingual yoga teacher, Reiki practitioner, motivational speaker, author and TV show host. She has been a teacher of teachers for over ten years, presenting at conferences and countries worldwide like Kripalu Center, Yoga Journal Live, Himalayan Institute, Omega Institute, Chile, Puerto Rico, Andorra, just to name a few. Rina is known as the yoga expert on Univision's Tu Desayuno Alegre and is an article contributor for Yoga Journal Online and MindBodyGreen. Rina is also a featured teacher on Gaiam TV's My Yoga Online. She has three Rina Yoga studios in the Miami area, including a partnership with the JW Marriott Marquis in Downtown Miami. She was selected as one of South Florida's Business Leaders  2011 Movers and Shakers, and teaches and speaks about marketing and entrepreneurship. Rina also created her own yoga app, Snooze Yoga, and a pioneering yoga curriculum for children and teens, Super Yogis' Schoolhouse.

She is known for her vibrant and uplifting approach to yoga. Never shy about herself, she understands that we are all the same and openly shares the lessons of her life without reservation, fostering an environment of complete trust. Warning: Her love of life is contagious.

FOREWORD

If you're picking up a book called 'Choose Peace,' then chances are some part of you doesn't feel fully at peace right now. This is ok! People are waking up to the fact that everything they've been told about how to find happiness may be wrong — and this can be tough to admit to ourselves. Maybe happiness is not something new to attain — maybe it's something always there, underneath our preconceptions of what it should be.

To actually confront the sources of our pain and remove them can be a daunting and scary process. In fact the initial stages can bring these sources to light, and often feel like the roof is coming down. But the methods described in Rina's book, although written in modern language, translate wisdom that has been tested for thousands of years. These issues, it seems, are universal and timeless, and these methods can reveal the peace that you have always had available. Like a muddy lake, to see the clear water that's always there, we can only wait and not disturb the water — and the mud will settle on its own.

So, if you give this a try, trust the process. The patterns in our minds form over years, and bringing them to light takes time. Trust and wait, and you will start to notice a shift in the way you feel. As Rainer Maria Rilke said,

"...I would like to beg you dear Sir, as well as I can, to have patience with everything unresolved in your heart and to try to love the questions themselves as if they were locked rooms or books written in a very foreign language. Don't search for the answers, which could not be given to you now, because you would not be able to live them. And the point is to live everything. Live the questions now. Perhaps then, someday far in the future, you will gradually, without even noticing it, live your way into the answer."

Jeff Lieberman
Artist, scientist, host of
'Time Warp' on Discovery Channel

PREFACE
Note to the Reader

Let me begin by mentioning that it is a pleasure to see you have decided to pick up this book. I hope you continue to use the book since it is meant to be used time and time again. In fact, I recommend you photocopy the exercises in the end of each chapter in order to maximize your use of the book and do the steps as many times as you want to.

Although my background is in yoga, I have tried to maintain the information in this book neutral and applicable to all. I use some analogies and terminologies learned from my yoga studies, but it is only meant to help you understand where I am coming from.

This book is an expression of my experience and how I came to where I am today. I have been asked about my credentials and my response is simple: I do not have a degree in psychology, but I have observed my own mind and behaviors plenty to have found a formula that helps me understand myself better in order to heal from within. Luckily, this formula has helped others heal as well. I have consulted with therapists, such as Dr. Brian Weiss, on the formula and they have approved of the method and some have expressed interest in sharing it with their clients. I feel that it is best for me to stay in the field of yoga. That's my strength! If at any point you feel that you need more consulting, please contact a local psychologist or alternative therapist.

ACKNOWLEDGEMENTS

There are many people that I would like to thank for making this book possible. One person cannot do it alone.

Special thanks go to Nina Paley for generously sharing your Mimi and Eunice comics from mimiandeunice.com, Virginia Benitez for your editing and your friendship, Wendy Long for proofreading, Tom Pratt for your tapas to life, Lauranda Hook for your creativity, Alexis Rua for your love, web-design, and consulting, James Joyner for your friendship and consulting, Maite Mendiola for your unconditional love and non-judgmental support, Heidy Toledo for your loyal assistance and dedication, Greg and Jane Faysash for your unconditional support and love, Jas'mine for riding our rollercoaster of sisterhood, Adrienne Ward for putting the wheels in motion, Michael Lerner for your advice and motivation, Carolina Rojas for asking me the most enlightening question, "What will maintain my peace?," Adriana Sol for the public relations and your lifelong friendship, Meryl Martin for your direct therapeutic help, Joan Varini for your dedication, Dr. Summer Sullivan for your psychological expertise, and last but never least, my Mom and Dad for providing assistance, support, unconditional love, and the unwavering belief in me from the very beginning of my life.

Oh! And, thank you for reading this book!

Introduction

*"Be careful with your thoughts,
for they become your words.
Be careful with your words,
for they become your actions.
Be careful with your actions,
for they become your habits.
Be careful with your habits,
for they become your character.
Be careful with your character,
for it becomes your destiny."*

– Anonymous

Welcome to the potential of seeing life with a new set of eyes and a new perspective. The original purpose of this book was to help a few of my private clients feel better during some hard times. I was having a difficult time explaining to them what seemed to make sense to me, so I decided to sit down and figure out exactly what had helped me heal through my own hard times. I sat down on a wooden bench one afternoon at a park and began to jot down a step-by-step process of what I had done to begin healing within just a year of what I would consider to be one of the lowest, if not the lowest, time of my life: my divorce. When I started to use the steps with some of my clients, I found that the formula seemed to work. So I gathered a few brave volunteers for more research, and much to my surprise, everyone, including me, seemed to suffer from the same common denominator: feeling rejected and not feeling accepted for being him/herself, thus, not feeling truly loved. My curiosity peaked. I began to see the same pattern in everyone I interacted with, and I felt I had to share this insight with everyone that would be willing to listen and do the work for him/herself.

In the following chapters, you will find 15 Steps, each with a description that helps facilitate the healing process. Therefore, the purpose of the book has evolved into a self-realizing workbook that guides you toward your own deeper healing and true inner peace.

Mia's Story

As an introduction to the workbook, I have written a brief story that explains how a character named Mia uses the steps in order to find her way towards realizing greater inner peace.

Mia is a woman who has experienced plenty of suffering. Although she knows there must be a way out of her suffering, she feels hopeless. She feels utterly defeated by life and doesn't know where to turn. She is 32 years old and works as an elementary school teacher. Her boyfriend just broke up with her, so she feels alone and abandoned.

Mia knows she needs to take care of herself by exercising, spending time with friends, continuing her dedication to her job, and eating healthy. But this, of course, is easier said than done. Her stress is causing her to lose her appetite, so she has lost a lot of weight, as well. She feels sadness and anger, lives in her own world, and suffers from a minor depression.

She doesn't know what to do. She knows she isn't happy, and with these negative emotions taking her over, she doesn't know how to begin to heal herself.

On her way home from work one day, she decides to stop by a bookstore to see if there were any useful self-help books. Instinctively, she picks up a journal at the store and walks over to the self-help section. She starts reading some titles, but nothing seems to grab her attention.

Nearby, a woman is observing Mia and approaches her. She asks her calmly "Do you need some help?" Mia assumes she works at the store, so she replies, "Yes, I am looking for a useful self-help book." The woman hands her a book with coiled binding with the title *Choose Peace: A Practical Guide into Consciousness.* Mia looks through the book and when she looks up to thank the woman, she is gone. Not thinking anything of it, Mia walks to the counter to pay for the book and the journal. The man behind the counter tells her that the book is not part of the store's inventory.

Confused, Mia remains quiet about the mysterious woman, while paying for the journal. She walks around the store to find the woman who gave her the book, but she is nowhere to be found.

When Mia gets home, she plops herself on her couch with a coffee in hand and looks out the window. She picks up her new book and thumbs through it curiously. The book is laid out into 15 steps with exercises which makes her think it might be too childish. She puts the book down and prepares some microwavable food. After unsuccessfully attempting to finish her dinner, she looks over at the book again and decides to give it a chance.

She pathetically says to herself, "What else do I have to

do tonight anyway?"

She sits down and begins reading the book again. She decides to trust the book and evaluate herself in order to see what would happen. She ponders, "What does she have to lose? Just this shitty feeling. It's a win-win."

The book suggests that the reader keep a journal in order to help him/her process the information deeper. She gives herself a pat on the back for listening to her intuition early at the bookstore. So, she grabs her journal too.

The first step poses the general question: "Are you at peace with your life?" Mia laughs and says, "Of course not, or I wouldn't be here reading this, would I?" Then she realizes she is talking to herself and laughs more.

The second step (Choose a Behavior, Any Behavior) asks her to define one of her behaviors. As she reads further, she takes some notes about what may have led to her recent breakup. After some time reflecting, she chooses the behavior and identifies it as "I have a difficult time making and maintaining deep, intimate, loving relationships because I push people away when they get too close."

In the third step (Charge of Behavior) she is asked if this behavior is positive (beneficial), negative (harmful), or neutral (has no effect). Although she believes that it could be harmful, she convinces herself that it could also be beneficial. So, she writes down both positive and negative. She moves on.

In the next step (Penny for Your Thoughts), she

pauses. She is asked to identify the thoughts behind her behavior. She asks herself, "What kinds of thoughts are they talking about?" She struggles with this step and decides to do the meditation exercise described in the book (see page 76) to help her find the answers. She sits up straight, grabs her journal and her pen. She sets her timer on her phone for ten minutes. She closes her eyes and begins her freestyle writing exercise with the thought of "I push people away" in her head, as the book suggests. After her timer goes off, she stops and reads her notes. She wrote down many things, but among them were, "I have no idea what to write. What am I supposed to be thinking about? This is silly." After these initial thoughts, she is able to find some answers.

She concludes that she feels it is better to push people away before they really get to know her for who she truly is. She wrote down in her journal, "I'm scared people won't like me for who I am so I prefer to push them away first before they push me away. I have to protect myself."

Intrigued, she continues with the steps. When the next step (Charge of Thoughts) asks her to identify whether these thoughts were positive, negative, or neutral, she chooses that her thoughts are both positive and negative. She feels her behavior keeps her from feeling peace, but it must serve her in some way or she wouldn't act that way. She figures it's a defense mechanism of some sort so she doesn't get hurt by others. She also realizes that she doesn't give people a chance and assumes they will push her away, so she just gets it over with faster. She frowns recognizing how unfortunate it is that she has acted this way her whole life and gets scared.

She questions whether or not to continue reading the book. She fears where this process might be taking her, but is also curious. With this confusion, she decides to go to bed and rest on what she has processed so far. It has been quite an eventful day for her.

The next morning before going to work, she grabs a cup of coffee and sees the book out of the corner of her eye. She remains a little distant from it, but she knows she has to continue the process. She is excited and cautious at the same time.

During her day at work, Mia forgets about the steps of the book. She immediately falls back into her thought patterns and gets distracted by teaching her students, grading papers, etc. Towards the middle of her day, one of the male teachers, Marco, comes up to her and asks her if she wants to get a coffee after work. She immediately panics and says, "No, I can't. I have a meeting I have to go to. But thanks." And walks away quickly. A little part of her was excited, but mostly she was scared. Truth is, she doesn't have a meeting and she does want to go with him but she figured he was feeling sorry for her or whatever other excuse she could think of to protect herself. The reality is he likes her and just wants to get to know her better. After school ends, she avoids seeing him and drives straight home.

Feeling a little anxious she chooses to pick up the book again in hopes of getting some answers. She grabs her journal first and opens it to refresh her memory a bit. She reads some of her thoughts she had written the day before. As she reads, she begins to think about how she just had a situation where she chose to not create a possible deep, intimate connection with someone out of fear. She clearly pushed Marco away before any emotions started brewing.

She is in amazement of how her behavior had just been revealed to her just a few hours ago. She has never noticed that before. This is the first time she can clearly see the parallel of her behavioral pattern disturbing her peace. She had been so lost in the situation she didn't notice herself in it. She surrenders her previous idea that her behavior and thoughts are partly positive because she isn't feeling the benefits.

She leans back in her chair now and takes a deep breath. She had no idea that this book could have lead her to such a deep place within herself so quickly. So with that intrigue, she keeps reading.

The next step (Broken Record in your Mind) asks her to identify her unconscious negative affirmation. A few examples are given in the book, although she has a hard time determining the affirmation at first. First she thinks it might be "I need to push everyone away." But she figures that might be too obvious. She then thinks "I can't connect." Neither of those resonate with her though, and she thinks the affirmation could be a little deeper especially since the book constantly reminds the reader not to choose superficial answers. She decides to do the meditation exercise once more, and these are some of the thoughts she wrote down: "What's wrong with running away?... I don't need anybody... Who would want

to be with me anyways?... I don't fit in... I'm different...
I don't even know how to connect intimately... I'm
unlovable... I'm undesirable... I'm not good enough...
I feel ugly..."

Since the step suggests to make the affirmation short
and to the point this is what Mia tries to achieve. After much
time pondering and feeling how each sentence resonates
with her, she chooses with reluctance of admitting this to
herself, "I am undesirable, unlovable, unaccepted, and
so different from everybody else." She sighs. She looks
up from her journal and sees the trees in front of her.
She feels the heaviness of feeling alone. She realizes that
this feeling of loneliness was created by her unconscious
choice to put up an imaginary barrier between herself
and everyone else. She gets up, goes to the bathroom
and washes a few tears off of her face. Although there
is no one there to see her cry, she can't allow herself to
show her sadness. She sits back down, takes a sip of her
coffee, and picks up the book again.

At this point, the book asks her to identify the
source of these thoughts and chosen affirmation (Whose
Thoughts are These?). Mia is a bit confused about this
step, so she reads further. The book explains that the
thoughts that go through your mind may not really
be yours. Some of them may come from your mother,
your father, the environment, society, friends, etc. As
humans, we pick up thoughts from others and make
them our own.

Mia decides to do the exercises at the end of the
chapter (see page 100). She writes down under the "source"

categories how these negative thoughts and her chosen affirmation relate to each other. This step takes some time. Mia decides to write out all of her thoughts in her journal as the book suggests. After a few days of soul searching, she discovers some very useful information.

Her stream-of-consciousness writing reveals the following: "I'm not sure why I withdraw from people... other than that is the way my family is and so it's what I learned growing up... we never shared our negative emotions... If we had problems we would just mind our own business... We wouldn't share... It was considered a weakness... And so I never connected with them deeply, only superficially... So indirectly I learned you can't trust people... you can't rely on others, they will always hurt you... that is what my family taught me... My source is also the past rejections which hurt my ego..."

Mia sees that some of her own characteristics resemble those of her mother's. Her parents have always taught her that she should never express or share her negative emotions, directly and indirectly. They would express verbally these concerns and of course, Mia would observe their behavior when they had negative emotions. Instead of expressing how they felt with clear communication, they would bottle it up and withdraw from each other. Hence, this is what she learned as well. "Holy shit," said Mia in amazement. "I'm one big puzzle. If I can piece the puzzle together, then I can see where I have been coming from all these years. And then hopefully I can lead myself consciously in another direction."

She reads on. In the next step (Effect of Thoughts),

Mia has to state whether the thoughts she has adopted from her family are beneficial or harmful. At this point, Mia accepts the truth. She writes down that they are harmful.

Then Mia is asked to identify the belief system that she has devised as a child in order to create this adopted defense mechanism (It's a Vicious Cycle). Mia asks herself, "What on earth is a belief system?"

She keeps reading and decides to write out her thoughts in her journal. What she understands to be one of her belief systems was the following: When she was a child, she gathered a lot of information. This information was processed in a few different ways. Either it was suppressed (concealed), repressed (pushed down), expressed (spoken), or discarded as unimportant. If she processed the information in one of the first three ways (suppressed, repressed or expressed) she had to learn how to adapt to it even if it was an unconscious reaction.

Mia understood that we, as children, react in a way that helps us create a belief system in order to survive in our given surroundings. If this is the right understanding, Mia concludes that she felt inadequate and rejected by her mother and father because they didn't allow her to express her emotions at a young age when everything is meant to be expressed freely. Therefore Mia, feeling inadequate, hid her true need and desire to be expressive, thinking that something was wrong with her. She pushed people away so that she wouldn't have to let them see that she was in pain. She didn't want to set herself up to be rejected as she had been by her own parents. Thus, she withdrew anytime she felt she had to defend herself in order to feel a false sense of security and safety. Her fear of being rejected or unloved drove her to feel that she had to protect herself from her surroundings. As a child she felt that if she showed she was unhappy or not in control of her feelings then she would not be accepted into the family. So she hid her feelings, put up a wall and maintained that defense mechanism her entire life without even being aware of it. In order to not feel the pain of rejection, she adopted a behavior that was approved by her family and she applied it to all similar situations in the future. All of this was unconscious, until now. Mia sighs.

After discovering this information, she takes a moment to regroup. These are a lot of emotions to feel and process. She feels a bit overwhelmed, so she gets up from the couch, grabs a glass of water, and goes to bed.

The next morning she wakes up exhausted. She remembers having vivid dreams, but can't detail any of them. Since it's Saturday, she has the whole day to continue reading and searching for more answers. She makes some toast and coffee (her regular easy-to-make meal) and sits down again on her couch.

Mia is on Step 10 (What is Truth?) where the author explains the difference between relative truth and absolute truth. Since these are new concepts to Mia, she thinks she might do some extra research. She begins searching online for articles on the topic. What she finds is insightful and interesting. At this point in the process, she is instructed to visualize her entire life as an illusion of relative truth and not the absolute truth that we all supposedly live in. Mia conceptualizes these ideas of the different truths and finds them challenging. She vows to keep figuring it out. She starts philosophizing by categorizing different ideas as either relative or absolute but is unable to understand the concept fully. She finally understands when she reads an example about how, in a series of factual events, three people can interpret three totally different stories depending on their views and perspective. After reading this, Mia remembers an incident when she had gone to court for an accident she was in. When the witnesses explained their sides of the story, she was amazed at how each person described a completely different scenario. She remembered thinking, "I need to communicate clearly, or it will seem as if I am lying." Then she remembered that each person completely believed their story, even though all three stories were different. This only meant that none of the stories were the truth, just the perspectives of the relative truths of each person observing the event.

Mia then sees the relative truth, also described as personal truth, in this particular behavior and story. As she keeps reading, her eyes become a little bigger and her body keeps getting pulled closer into the book. She reads the whole chapter and then stops. She verbally repeats some of the ideas given in order to make it click in her head. After talking to herself about it for a while and writing some ideas down in her journal, she decides to move onto the next step, although she doesn't completely grasp the connection She figures it might come in time, so she moves on.

In Step 11 (Change Your Mind) the reader is asked to come up with a conscious positive affirmation to serve as a counter attack on the reader's unconscious negative affirmation identified in Step 6 (Broken Record in your Mind). Mia remembers that her unconscious, negative affirmation was "I am undesirable, unlovable, unaccepted, and so different from everybody else.". She has to come up with a positive one. She thought of a few possible choices such as, "I am good enough... I am not unloved... I don't need to withdraw... I'm not different," but none of those options resonated. She did a few of the exercises provided in the book and realized that she was choosing phrases that still had the word *not* in them. She is advised against this, so she finds some better options were, "I accept love into my life," "I express my emotions in a healthy way," and "I am loved." She ends up choosing this one: "I love and accept myself therefore I welcome others into my life." In all honesty, she feels weird and uncomfortable saying it to herself and slouches her body, protecting her heart when she says it. But she knows she will need to get more comfortable repeating it so she might as well start now.

Mia starts to feel great about the whole process. She is feeling quite proud of herself for how much she has accomplished and learned about herself in these few days. Proud and inspired, Mia reads on.

Her inspiration and pride draws to a halt when Mia reads the next step. She gets stumped. Just the title scares her an makes resist.

Step 12 (Forgive Yourself) urges Mia to find forgiveness and compassion towards herself and her story, which according to the book, is much easier to accomplish once she mostly understands and experiences the difference between relative truth and absolute truth. Mia starts to get frustrated with the whole formula and puts the book aside. She was feeling great before because she had tackled so many of the steps, but now she feels that she can't go any further. She doesn't like the feeling of defeat–that she can't go on–so she neglects the book for a few weeks. Her feeling of inadequacy ("I'm not good enough") prevents her from going further in the steps because she wasn't ready to go deeper through the healing process for now.

The several weeks that she is away from the book doesn't mean that Mia stops healing. In fact, it was the exact opposite. Because she left the book for a while, her mind starts to observe the things that she had already noted in the previous steps. She becomes more aware of her patterned behavior and reminds herself of the positive affirmation ("I love and accept myself therefore I welcome others into my life.") as soon as she hears the negative one ("I am undesirable, unlovable and unaccepted and so different from everybody else") in her head. Naturally, there are times that she doesn't remember, and she gets caught up in her mini-drama leading her to feel scared, angry and frustrated. As a reaction to this she spends hours upset but then eventually pauses and observes her thoughts. She recalls her affirmation, "I love and accept myself therefore I welcome others into my life." She begins using other positive affirmations when needed, also realizing their power. She starts instinctually using the one affirmation that resonates the most at any particular moment.

She is beginning to be sensitive to her own story and to her own true emotions. She even starts becoming sensitive to other people's emotions, and she begins observing their behaviors.

One day at school, Mia is talking to one of her students named Tommy.   Tommy is one of those students who always hands in his homework on time and gets high grades. He is polite, kind, studious, and smart, but he usually has a hard time making friends. When Mia notices that he has missed his homework assignments a few days in a row, she knows that something is going on with him. The next day, Mia asks Tommy for the homework assignments he has missed for that week. Tommy responds, "I don't have them." Mia reacts unconsciously since this was the third time this has happened that week. She scolds him in front of his peers saying, "Tommy, speak to me after class! This is unacceptable!"

Andrew, one of Tommy's classmates, turns around in his chair and gives Tommy a high five. Tommy smiles and laughs. Mia finds this to be very strange. Andrew is one of the more popular students, and although he is smart too, he doesn't care as much about grades and school as Tommy does. She has never seen them interacting before.   Then,   she pauses and notices her reaction earlier towards Tommy. She had felt frustrated, so she lashed out in her own way. She repeats the affirmation, "I love and accept myself therefore I welcome others into my life.", and takes a deep breath. Otherwise, she would react by pushing Tommy away with harsher words and anger since he is acting in a way that challenges her worth as a teacher.

After class, she calls Tommy up to her desk. Tommy is a bit nervous because he's not used to getting in trouble. All of the students are gone from the class, and Mia sits him down next to her. She begins by asking him, "What has been going on?" "Why?", Tommy asks, puzzled. She calmly replies, repeating her affirmation in her head, "You have not been turning in your homework assignments, and this doesn't seem to be like you. Is something going on at home or at school?" He tries to give her the run around, but she feels that she knows what is going on. She asks him kindly and compassionately, "Are you acting rebellious so that you can be accepted by other students like Andrew?" She gives him an endearing face. Tommy looks up at his teacher and nods with an ashamed look.

Mia pauses as she discovers a rare gem that has been hidden inside her for a long time: her intuition. She has never been able to see so clearly how someone's actions can be completely driven by the basic need to be accepted and loved by others. She is flabbergasted and is now able to show genuine compassion for Tommy, since she has been in a similar situation even if in a different way.

"A different way!" Mia exclaims in her head. She

excitedly writes down the phrase on a piece of paper so she won't forget her moment of awareness, but she has to deal with the situation at hand.

After Tommy leaves the classroom, Mia takes out a piece of paper and on the top writes the words, "A DIFFERENT WAY!" She begins to process her thoughts. "Tommy is just looking for acceptance just like I did and still do. Although we may achieve it in different ways (relative truth) we are still seeking the same outcome. And, most of the time it is completely unconscious. Luckily I am able to reach out to Tommy early in his life while he is creating his belief system. Even if he doesn't understand, at least I know that I am able to see his belief system in action and help him consciously without reactions or fears. This fear of not being accepted or loved drove us both to act out in different ways, unconsciously. This only hurts us and doesn't benefit us. If we can just accept and love who we are, then everything would be a lot easier. Then, I am sure I will find peace. How do I get to that point? This is really amazing. I feel like I have put together a bit more of my puzzle. Tommy and I process the information differently, but we both are looking for acceptance and love from others."

Mia rushes home and picks up the book again. She has experienced Steps 10 (What is Truth?) and 13 (Nothing is Personal) without even realizing it. She is ready for more.

That day had been a truly experiential moment of truth for her. She is ready and the universe has graced her with knowledge and wisdom. She is extremely grateful.

Introduction to the Steps

*"The poor long for riches,
the rich long for heaven, but
the wise long for a state of
tranquility."*

– Swami Rama

Everybody has a different rock bottom. For me, it was my divorce. I was tired of suffering from the divorce, so I decided I needed to take control of my life and change it positively if I wanted to have a different outcome for my life. This situation is what led me to discover these steps, which helped me find some peace. But of course, every person is different, therefore, so is his or her healing process. After doing these steps with several case studies, I have found that they can be highly effective and efficient. These steps are not meant to be a quick fix. If you are expecting to take a pill and be healed, then this is not the book for you. I have found though, that these steps can have a lasting effect and hopefully they will for you. But, I will not lie, you have to put forth a lot of effort to make the changes you want in your life and be brave enough to venture into unknown and possibly dark areas that lie deep below the surface. It's not only about having positive thoughts and thinking that you will be great–you have to take the actions to get you there as well. This book will take you from an understanding of your physical behavior towards the deeper hidden belief behind that behavior, so that if you choose to, you can change your reality.

I have provided a 15-Step formula that will help you process why you do the things you do. Once you can apply that understanding to one part of your life, do another, and you will see how easy it is to break everything down into this formula. It's a systematic approach to healing yourself with clear guidelines, tools, and directions. If you get stuck at moments, that is normal. Don't force the process. The moment you do, you will need to pause and observe yourself a bit more.

The reason I refer to the process as a formula is because I feel that if you add X (you) + Y (your unconscious negative habit/behavior), you will get S (pain and suffering), which can be harmful for you. A change in formula to X + W (a new conscious positive behavior) can equal P (peace and happiness.) The formula is simple, but it is important to put this formula into action so that we can see the results and how it can benefit us.

There are a few approaches and mentalities that will help you pass through these steps more efficiently.

First, be honest with yourself. Even if it seems painful at first, do it and see what happens. Don't be afraid to go deep with your answers. If your answers are superficial, then your healing will also be superficial. Second, be patient with yourself. You may get frustrated that you have not found an answer to one of these steps. That is natural, just take it one step at a time and be as present as you can be through the process. There will be times that you will rise and fall and rise again. Know that this process is not going to change you overnight but over time. Listen to your gut as much as you can. It is constantly telling you the truth, so listen to it whenever you can. Also, don't add any judgment towards yourself. It may be a conditioned reaction to judge yourself as good or bad, but refrain from doing so as much as possible. You might be judgmental towards yourself and others. It's a powerful behavior so be aware of it if it surfaces during this process.

Write out as much as you can on a separate sheet of paper when doing these steps. It is helpful to buy a journal specifically for this book so you can keep your thoughts clear. Write all of the things that come to your mind. Don't edit yourself. Don't be attached to any of your answers. Be open and notice your moments of attachment and clinging. You will need to put your ego - the part of you that identifies with, labels and judges yourself or others - aside for this process. If you find yourself using your ego for a lot of these steps, observe those moments. In the ancient yoga scriptures called the yoga sutras of Patanjali, sutra (teaching) 12 of book 1 states that in order to begin to control the mind and its thought forms, one must use two main approaches during one's process; constant practice and nonattachment. Keep these two approaches in mind while you go further into your search for inner peace, and recall that nonattachment does not mean indifference.

Use the Case Studies at the end of the book as a reference and helpful guide to see the range of possible answers. Use the 15-Step Table (page 184) to help you organize your thoughts. Using the table will help you condense the answers in as few words or sentences as possible. Write out all of your thoughts and emotions in your journal first. This will take some time, but be patient and apply all of the other useful tips mentioned before. The exercises at the end of each chapter are there to help guide you in the right direction. It is important that you go step by step and not jump around. You can always stop while working on one step and take your time processing the material. There is no need to rush through this book. You will begin to see your unconscious reactions turn to conscious actions, which in turn will have you choosing inner peace.

The Steps

"Peace of mind is attained not by ignoring problems, but by solving them."

– Raymond Hull

Review and read through all of the steps in this chapter in order to get a feel for the journey you are about to begin. Don't get stuck in analyzing one step while reading this outline format. Continue reading the book in order to get more information and explanations about each step.

Please notice that in some of these steps, I use the word identify, instead of observe. Identify implies observing and also acting. You must observe first in order to be able to identify. In your stages of observation, you are writing in your journal and sorting through your emotions and thoughts. In your stages of identification, you will read through your observations and then choose the most appropriate response and action that best resonates your truth. Therefore, technically when I write identify, I am meaning, observe, then identify. Once you can identify the conclusion, then that means you have observed and contemplated the step thoroughly.

Below is a brief overview of the fifteen steps.

Step 1: Have Inner Peace?

Observe and answer these questions: Are you at peace? Are you happy?

Have you always wanted to heal a certain area of your life, but didn't know how to start?

Have you felt hopeless about a certain situation that seems to happen over and over again in your life? Have you ever wondered why you feel and act the way you do?

Step 2: Choose a Behavior, Any Behavior

Identify only one of your behaviors.

Step 3: Charge of Behavior

Identify whether this behavior is positive (beneficial), negative (harmful), and/or neutral (non-effecting.)

It is important to consider that you are distinguishing the effect of the behavior and not you as a person, so don't add any judgment of good or bad.

Step 4: Penny for Your Thoughts

Identify the thoughts behind your behavior.

Step 5: Charge of Thoughts

Identify whether these thoughts are positive, negative, and/or neutral.

Don't add judgment of good or bad.

Step 6: Broken Record in Your Mind

Identify your unconscious affirmation. Make the affirmation consistent with your thoughts identified in Step 4 (Penny for your Thoughts).

Step 7: Whose Thoughts are These?

Identify the source of your thoughts, i.e. mom, dad, family, school, friends, yourself, news, society, etc. Don't place blame once you identify the source(s).

Step 8: Effect of Thoughts

Identify whether these thoughts are beneficial or harmful to you.

Don't add judgment here either.

Step 9: It's a Vicious Cycle

Identify your belief system developed in childhood regarding these thoughts.

This is some serious soul searching. You must go deep and be transparent here.

Step 10: What is Truth?

Discover that the belief system was created from your relative (personal) truth at that specific time using your ego and a need to protect yourself. Discover the difference between these relative truths and the absolute truths of the universe as they pertain to your daily life.

Step 11: Change your Mind

Recall your unconscious negative affirmation from Step 6 (Broken Record in Your Mind). Change it to a conscious positive affirmation.

Step 12: Forgive Yourself

Find forgiveness and compassion for yourself and your past actions since they were relative to certain circumstances and you weren't as aware or conscious as you are now. Understand that it's just your story, but not you. It's what you needed to go through in order to be here now and question yourself and your life. You've come to the point of searching for healing through this book.

Step 13: Nothing is Personal

Discover that everyone else's actions are also based on their relative truths and see how their belief systems may have brought them to act a certain way towards life and towards you. Therefore, how a person acts towards you is never personal. It's his/her own story.

Step 14: Forgive Others

Find forgiveness and compassion for everyone else and his/her story, because they are suffering just like you are. Also, this compassion is important because he/she may not be on the same healing path as you, and unfortunately, he/she will continue to suffer due to ignorance of the difference between relative and absolute truth.

Step 15: Practicing the Process

Now, let's put this all together and put it into practice.

When confronted with a situation that stirs up negative thoughts, affirmations and behaviors, stop and remind yourself of the relative truth behind your belief system that has triggered these before and overcome them by changing your thoughts and actions in that moment in order to be in harmony with how you truly feel. Begin by repeating a positive affirmation whenever you notice a harmful one habitually and unconsciously repeating itself. This last step is a never-ending process.

Please go to the Appendix and photocopy the 15-Step Table provided on page 180.

In the following chapters I'll elaborate on each one of these steps and give examples.

Step 1

Have Inner Peace?

"Set peace of mind as your highest goal, and organize your life around it."

– Brian Tracy

What does inner peace mean to you? To me, inner peace can have many different levels, but in general it implies that I am acting in conjunction with my thoughts (my head), my feelings (my heart), and my intuition in order to connect with my deeper purpose and significance in this universe in a state of tranquility, flow, and serenity based on my understanding of absolute truth. This definition works for me and is always able to be changed and modified. You will most likely have your own definition that works better for you. And if you haven't thought about it, take a few moments to think about it now.

The first question you must ask yourself is, generally: "Am I at peace with my life?" Most people will quickly answer this question and say, "Sure, I'm fine." But after reading this book and going inwards a bit, you might realize that there are still things you might want to heal. You might be at peace in some areas of your life, but maybe not in others. Those areas that are not in peace are the ones to focus on for this book. Just the fact that you are reading this book means you are looking for more inner peace, so this step could be quite simple to answer since it is a yes or no question.

Additional useful questions to answer would be:

"Am I happy?"

"Do I feel stuck or stagnant in a certain area of my life?"

"Do I feel comfortable in my own skin?"

"Do I find it difficult to stay grounded?"

"Do I suffer from depression?"

"Do I feel like a victim?"

"Do I feel complacent, tired, or lost in my life?"

"Do I constantly dwell in the past?"

"Am I constantly worried about the future?"

These are all questions that will hopefully help you see where you are right now in your life. Before you can maintain your peace, you have to have the right map in order to find it. And that is exactly what this book's intention is: to give you a road map towards your inner peace.

If you feel like one or some of these questions touch upon or reveal something that you are going through, then you might want to take a moment to venture into the second step which will mark the beginning of a healing journey for you. This is not for the faint of heart. It takes a true warrior and a courageous person to embark on this journey into the self. This is a warning for all who feel they might not be ready for this kind of healing in their lives. You'll know if you are ready. And if you don't know, then keep reading and there might be a point when you may need to stop. You will know then, like Mia did, and if that time comes for you, please listen to your intuition.

At the beginning of this process, you might feel some negative and dark emotions come up, which is a good sign. We all have these dark places, but for some reason we as a society think we can hide from such places and pretend they don't exist. In fact, everyone has these dark places and if we don't expose them, then we will never be free from them. With some determination and proper guidance, you can begin to heal those wounds that have been pestering you for most of your life. You may even discover others you have repressed for a long time. This first step is the beginning of your process toward clarity. What do you have to lose? It's a wonderful journey and I myself have experienced many changes by implementing these steps in my own life. I am giving you the formula that helped me through one of the hardest years of my life. I hope it helps you as much as it has helped me.

If you are ready to go to the next step, I commend you on your bravery. Know that this isn't something that all people are willing to do, so congratulations on your decision to choose conscious living, health, and healing. If you are not ready to embark on this journey yet, it's ok. Don't judge yourself. I surely do not. I know this is a hard decision and when you are ready, you will know. This book might happen to fall into your lap again one day, and you will know that it is time.

So, if the book has fallen into your lap again and you are ready for this journey, let's begin. Remember, you will have moments of inspiration and moments when you fall; it is a cycle of ups and downs and picking yourself

up again. Don't beat yourself up if you happen to fall a
few times; that is natural and happens to everyone. So,
enter this journey without expectations and you will find
it even more rewarding. I know it is easier said than done,
but at least attempt it. Life isn't about your mistakes, it's
about your experiences and whether you dwell on them
negatively or learn from them and keep growing.

So, are you ready to learn about yourself and keep
growing?

Throughout this book, we are going to follow Mia's
story in certain cases in order to see how she dealt with
each step on her own. When asked if she was at peace,
Mia stated that she wasn't at peace since she felt lonely
after her break-up with her boyfriend and for other
reasons as well.

Step 1 Exercises

Inner Peace Definition Exercise

What does inner peace mean to you?

_____
_____
_____
_____

Are you living peacefully?

_____
_____
_____
_____

What Disturbs my Peace Exercise

Do this exercise as many times as you need to. Take your time. Your answers can be anything, simple or complex. Please fill in the blanks below.

One thing that disturbs my peace is

_____
_____
_____
_____

Another thing that disturbs my peace is

_____
_____
_____
_____

Another thing that disturbs my peace is

_____
_____
_____
_____

Another thing that disturbs my peace is

_____
_____
_____
_____

Another thing that disturbs my peace is

_____
_____
_____
_____

Do I have Inner Peace?

_____
_____
_____
_____

Step 2

Choose a Behavior,
Any Behavior

*"I do not want the peace which
passeth understanding, I want the
understanding which bringeth peace."*

– Helen Keller

The second step is to identify one of your behaviors. A behavior is an action that you do on a regular basis that has become a part of your personality and character. Choose something simple and easy to start. Remember to only choose one behavior at a time so you stay focused and refrain from getting your mind cluttered.

In this step, it is most beneficial to observe one particular action, habit, or behavioral pattern in your life. Choose a physical behavior that anyone can see you are doing. This will make it easier for you to tangibly work with the steps. Once you observe this behavior, then identify it by saying it aloud and writing it down. Identifying something implies an action behind your observing. You can be a keen observer, but if you don't make a choice to identify a behavior then you are not owning up to it and instead, you're remaining passive. This process is a very active one. It requires your undivided attention. I know this can get exhausting, but just keep on working. The exhaustion is part of the process as well.

This step is very important because by choosing an action in this way, you are taking responsibility for this action and realizing it as something to identify, not just observe. Again, this process is extremely active, and if you are going to start passively, then it won't work so well. This formula works best when you are frustrated with the recurring negative situations in your life and you are open to change.   Another thing you will notice about the examples provided is that I am not using the words "I like" or "I hate." These imply desires and are not specific to just the behavior.   Edit your answer until it is short and sweet. Get rid of all the superfluous information, judgments, and excuses you say to yourself and get right down to the core of the behavior from the beginning. This will make the rest of your journey much smoother. If you notice you can't be honest or truthful with yourself then consider this trait to be your first behavior. Merely write down "trouble being honest and truthful with myself." Don't choose a behavior just because it sounds right or easy. Choose a behavior that might be hard for you to say aloud and admit. That behavior will be the most impactful.

I will give you a few examples in order to help you figure out which way to go. Notice that at times I use the phrase "too much" or "too little." Please make sure that when you write this out you are not placing judgment. This behavior you choose is based on your feelings about where you are in life, according to you, not according to other people's expectations. Do not choose a behavior that your mom reminds you of daily like "Don't drag your feet. Don't slouch." This could imply that you would choose the behavior of "bad posture."   In all of my examples I have placed neither the word "bad" nor "good." I have kept them general and nonjudgmental. Do the same with your behavior. Catch yourself if you write these judgmental statements down or say them aloud often. If you write, for example, "I drink too much," then that should be because you have noticed that the behavior is starting to be detrimental to your life, but not because someone else tells you so.

I would like to take a moment to explain a very important teaching I learned from Raja Yoga; the eight limbs of yoga. The first limb talks about the five virtues that you want to cultivate in your life with regards to how you relate to the outside world, called the yamas. One of the five yamas is asteya, non-stealing. This virtue of non-stealing is not only talking about not physically stealing a possession that doesn't belong to you, but also about not stealing someone or something else's energy. According to science, all animate and inanimate objects are made up of energy. Although we seem solid, there are little atoms that are moving around constantly inside of us and around everything. There are two energies that permeate our bodies. One is the life force energy that is constant and permanent in everyone and everything. This life force energy comes from within us and is connected to our higher self or the Pure Self, which will be discussed later in the book. It is our source of infinite supply of energy.

The other form of energy is increased, maintained or decreased by outside or external sources. It is easier to manipulate and control unconsciously or consciously.

We can get boosts of energy from a variety of external sources, like eating, drinking alcohol, talking with friends, engaging with family, doing drugs, having sex, gossiping, exercising, doing yoga, watching a movie, listening to music, reading a book, taking a bath, getting a massage, playing a game, flirting, working, drawing, dancing, creating, writing, judging, singing, competing, etc. Since our source of energy is provided by something or someone else then it is temporary. At this point you might be wondering how this is correlated with stealing, but let's take a moment to think about how if this external source of energy is not our energy, then we are taking it from somewhere or something else. It doesn't belong to you. It is borrowed. Therefore, we need to decide which sources of energy we will borrow energy from healthily and unhealthily. The behaviors that we tend to do habitually are behaviors that provide us with some sort of temporary energy because we are using that sources energy to boost ourselves momentarily. So, take this into consideration when choosing a behavior for this step. Observe the effects of doing different behaviors to find the one that may provide you with an unhealthy jolt of energy from something or someone else. Be honest with yourself.

If you are having trouble thinking of your behavior, here are some examples. Some of these examples have been expressed during my case studies. They may not all seem to be physical behaviors, but if you analyze closely they are because although some may start mental, like judging or manipulating other, eventually they require you to physically act by using words to express yourself.

Not being able to say no
Manipulating others
Being violent
Putting everyone else first at my expense
Always putting myself first at the expense of others
Excessive drinking
Smoking cigarettes
Needing constant attention
Being judgmental towards others and/or myself
Having extreme mood swings
Withdrawing from society
Talking excessively
Excessively needing sex
Not exercising enough or exercising too much
Eating too much or too little
Acting like a victim
Aggressive driving
Excessive drug use
Watching too much television
Sleeping too much or too little
Cleaning the house excessively
Never bathing
Laughing out of nervousness
Not taking anything seriously
Needing to control everything
Wanting to change people
Not allowing others to help me
Trouble opening up to people

Feeling bored when I speak to people

Being too hard on myself

Letting people walk all over me

Complaining too much or too little

Expressing my opinion too much or too little

Not trusting people

Being too trusting of people

There are plenty of options, but I hope you understand what you need to do first. This will set the tone for the rest of the steps.

Sit down and think about what habits or actions keep you from being at peace with yourself. You could also just choose any habit that you experience the majority of the time. Be honest with yourself here. You have nothing to lose, so dare to be open and truthful. See what happens. Use yourself as an experiment. Use your journal to write it all down and help you organize yourself. Refer to the exercise in the previous chapter in order to help you see what disturbs your peace. Then use the 15-Step Table on page 180 to write down the simplified version of your behavior. Use the table to remain organized and clear with your thoughts.

If you are getting overwhelmed and can't think of a behavior, do the meditation exercise on page 57. Use this exercise whenever you feel stuck in any step. It is highly effective in sorting out your thoughts.

Mia chose the following behavior: "I have a difficult time developing deep, intimate, loving connections with people because I push them away."

Step 2 Exercises

Meditation Exercise

Sit down comfortably in a quiet place either on the floor or in a chair. Keep your spine straight and long. Grab a pen and paper and place it on your lap. Sit tall with your eyes closed and begin to write down anything and everything that pops into your mind. Don't edit anything that comes up. Be raw so that you can get it all out on paper. Don't worry about staying in the lines; just write, even if it's on top of the previous writing. (However, have it somewhat legible for yourself at the end.)

Do this for ten minutes.

Once you are done, put down the pen, and read what you wrote. Notice if there are common themes in your writings. Write them below. Then you can start to see where your tendencies lay, and that lead you to your habits. Usually the most pressing thing in your life at the moment is what you need to heal the most. Go with it. Don't fight the process. Listen and be receptive. This will help you a lot.

Theme Exercise

Theme 1

_____

_____

_____

Theme 1

_____

_____

_____

Theme 1

_____

_____

_____

Now, circle the one that most resonates.

What will Maintain my Peace Exercise

In this exercise, I want you to think of five decisions you made today or yesterday. These decisions can be anything, for example, what you decided to eat for a meal, what you did after work, where you went to use the restroom, who you saw after work, when you took a shower, if you answered a phone call, how you spoke to a co-worker, if you called a friend, if you flirted with someone, what you wore, etc. Every action you make is a decision, so just choose five for now.

Decision 1:

_____

_____

_____

Decision 2:

_____

_____

_____

Decision 3:

_____

_____

_____

Decision 4:

_____

_____

_____

Decision 5:

_____

_____

_____

Now, take these five decisions and think back to the moment before you made each of those decisions. Close your eyes and think. Did you make the decisions based on what would benefit you the most in terms of maintaining inner peace, or based on a habit, reaction, or pattern? Next to each decision, I would like you to write MP for Maintained Peace or HR for Habit and Reaction. MP basically implies that you consciously made a decision based on the fact that you knew it would make you feel a sense of inner peace as its effect. HR implies that it was a decision you made because you are used to doing it–of giving in consistently–as though the action might give you peace, but instead it gives you only temporary pleasure. Inner peace is more constant (although nothing is permanent.) Your unconscious habits and reactions trick you into believing that they are beneficial for you in the short term, but in fact they usually are not in the long term.

Next, think about how your decision might have changed if you had paused and asked yourself the question, "In this situation, what will maintain my peace?" Then write the alternative decision below for each respective decision above. If you don't know, that is fine. Be honest with yourself and see what pops up in your mind and heart. The rest of this book will help you find some answers that suit you well. Sri Swami Satchidananda's translation of Patanjali's Yoga Sutras states that many of us are selfish in this life, which he states is ok as long as the only thing we are selfish about is maintaining our inner peace. He encourages us to make all our decisions based on that key component, which allows us to flow with the tide and not fight it, or, suffer.

Alternative Decision 1:

_____

_____

_____

Alternative Decision 2:

_____

_____

_____

Alternative Decision 3:

_____

_____

_____

Alternative Decision 4:

_____

_____

_____

Alternative Decision 5:

_____

_____

_____

My one behavior is

_____

_____

_____

_____

Step 3

Charge of Behavior

*"Those who are at war with others are
not at peace with themselves."*

– William Hazlett

Once you have established only one behavior, then identify whether this behavior is positive, negative, and/or neutral. The charge of your behavior is being associated with the electrical charges of positive negative and/or neutral. But in this context, positive means that the habit benefits your life, negative means that the habit is detrimental or harmful to you, and neutral means that it is neither beneficial nor harmful and has no effect on your life.

Don't judge whether the habit is good or bad. This will not be helpful for you during this process because it causes many negative emotions and you will feel more attached and emotionally invested in the process. We want to have a level of nonattachment through the process in order to be able to assess ourselves subjectively, as Patanjali suggests in the yoga sutras. This formula is meant to help you put the puzzle pieces together. If you remain judgmental, then there is an automatic barrier between you and your inner peace. Judgment is something the ego enjoys. The ego makes you feel better than or worse than someone or something else. There is more about the ego in Chapter 10. For the maximum benefit of this process, eliminate any judgment or comparison between yourself and others. If you find this difficult, then the behavioral pattern of "being judgmental" would be an appropriate one for you to choose in order to process these 15 Steps. See if this resonates with you. If not, continue with your original behavior.

Assume that one of my actions is that I have to wash my clothes once a week. This action might be negative if I place a lot of burden on myself over it and complain the whole time, since I feel I shouldn't have to wash my clothes. It might be positive because I get satisfaction from cleaning my clothes and feel like I've accomplished something. It could be a neutral action if I just wash my clothes since I know I have to wear them the next day without placing any emotions or reactions and accept it. I don't have an opinion about it nor does it affect my life positively or negatively.

Using the example of Mia, she said that her behavior was positive and negative. To recall, her behavior was "I have a difficult time developing deep, intimate, loving connections with people because I push people away." In regards to the charge of her behavior, she said, and this is a direct quote: "My behavior keeps me from feeling at peace, but it must serve me in some way or I wouldn't use it. I guess it's a defense mechanism." Some behaviors will seem to be both positive and negative.

Most people know instantly which answer it is, meaning that this step may not take long one to figure out, but you may need to use the exercises below to help you. You may be surprised by your answers. The simpler the information the easier it is for you to stay clear.

Step 3 Exercises

To find out which charge your behavior is, fill in the
following statements.

My behavior benefits me because:

_____
_____
_____
_____

My behavior hurts me because:

_____
_____
_____
_____

My behavior doesn't affect me at all because:

_____
_____
_____
_____

Using the space below just write the word(s) Positive,
Negative, and/or Neutral.

Charge(s) of Behavior is/are

_____
_____

Step 4

Penny for Your Thoughts

*"Who lives in harmony with himself
lives in harmony with the world."*

– Marcus Aurelius

This step is one of the most important in the beginning of this process. At this point, you need to identify the thoughts that provoke the habitual behavior or action. Don't edit yourself. It is imperative that at this point you have no fear in being honest and true to yourself. You can use the same meditation exercise previously explained in Step 2, focusing on the behavior identified in order to seek deeper meaning and information. This will show you exactly what your thoughts are towards this action. You are finding out what leads up to the recurring action or behavior, so you must start by looking at your thoughts.

Another technique would be to notice the words you use and how you express yourself verbally. Since we speak what we think, this could help you identify further. Notice how often you say "no" or any negative words or emotions. Begin to notice if you tend to be more negative or positive with your words. Most likely, if your words are negative, your thoughts are negative.

Write all your thoughts down. You will probably find a common theme. Stick with it. Refrain from being superficial in this step. Your initial thoughts might be ones that you could talk about with anyone that asks, but go deeper. Keep asking yourself, "What am I feeling?" Formulate the words so that they hit you in a deeper place. Choose words of truth that you can't avoid once they resonate. If you can't seem to do this at this step, don't get frustrated. It's ok. You might get to the heart of it at a later step. Again if you are doing this and thinking to yourself, " I have to do this right" and beating yourself up about it, then you might want to make that your behavior to tackle. Your behavior could simply be, "I tend to be too hard on myself." Then go from there. You don't need to start over with the table, but you could. You will know what is best for your process. A lot of these answers connect to deeper truths about yourself so be aware of the web of information that you might discover.

I promise you, once you start to go deeper, the answers will come up. They have been waiting to be revealed. Don't be afraid, and trust that everything will be ok. It might feel a bit painful at the beginning, but you are already in pain, so just allow it to come out a little more. This way you can be clear of it soon and heal more smoothly.

Let me give you an example from a different case study. A woman said that her thoughts were that she felt she didn't work hard enough at her job in order to deserve an award she got recently. She felt she was only going through the motions at her job. So, I asked her, "Do you feel you are not worthy of the award?" She sadly said yes. So I said that maybe her thoughts go a bit deeper -

like she feels that she is less than worthy in general and that she doesn't deserve anything in a symbolic sense. She paused for a few moments, reflected, and replied with an astonished, "Yes – wow!" So her statement at the beginning was a bit cluttered superficially by just stating she felt badly at work for receiving an award that she felt she didn't deserve. When we pressed further, we found a deeper truth and emotion within her that had been dormant. So, when I said that statement above, she saw how I was going deeper into the truth and I resonated with her in a more hidden place where her truest feelings and emotions lived. This is what I mean about diving deep for your answers from the beginning of the process. You might not be able to do this right off the bat, but see how far you are willing to go. Most likely, if you are writing scholarly academic answers, then you won't get as far as you could if you put on a "childlike voice." Put yourself in the mind of a child and talk and feel like a child. Answering these questions with a childlike mind will help you a lot. Attempt it and see what happens.

Mia defined her behavior "I can't seem to develop deep, intimate, loving connections with people." She revealed that her thoughts were that her "problems originate from childhood traumas of not being desirable. I still fear the rejection."

Once you have figured out all of your thoughts regarding your behavior on a separate piece of paper or journal, then write down the general theme on the 15-Step Table provided.

Step 4 Exercises

Meditation Exercise

This exercise is similar to the first meditation exercise except you are focusing on your thoughts behind one particular behavior.

So, sit down comfortably in a quiet room, either on the floor or in a chair. Keep your spine straight and long. Grab a pen and paper and place it on your lap. Sit tall with your eyes closed and begin to write down anything and everything that pops into your mind regarding this one behavior. Refrain from editing anything that comes up. Be raw so that you can get it all out on paper. Don't worry about staying in the lines; just write, even if it's on top of the previous writing. (However, have it somewhat legible for yourself at the end.)

Do this for ten minutes. Even if the time seems long and tedious, keep writing for ten minutes. A lot of things will come out that you might have never discovered.

Once you are done, put down the pen, and read what you wrote. Notice if there are common thoughts in your writings. Then you can start to see what your consistent thoughts are, which lead you to your habits. Don't fight the process. Listen and be receptive. This will help you a lot.

My thoughts are

_____
_____
_____
_____
_____
_____
_____

Theme Exercise

Below, write down a theme you discovered about your thoughts when it comes to your behavior. These could be anything and in any form like mental, emotional, in the form of questions, concerns, do you use past tense, present tense, future tense for your sentences, and the use of common words in your daily vocabulary like 'no', 'can't', 'I', 'me', 'should', 'could have', 'why,' etc. All of these themes will help you learn more about your perceptions in life right now. Usually they help tap into what works and what doesn't work for you.

Theme 1

_____
_____
_____

Theme 1

_____
_____
_____

Theme 1

_____
_____
_____

Step 5

Charge of Thoughts

*"Nothing can bring you peace,
but yourself."*

– Ralph Waldo Emerson

Once again, in this step we are going to correlate the electrical charges of positive, negative and neutral with the charges and effects of your thoughts. Just as electrical charges don't have judgments placed on them nor are they good or bad, don't place any judgments here regarding your thoughts. Good or bad is relative to each person. What is right for me may be wrong for someone else. Just like what is good for me might be bad for someone else. So adding judgment is irrelevant for this step. Therefore, identify if these thoughts are beneficial, harmful, or not affecting.

If you identified your behavior as both positive and negative, then in this step, you should determine which is stronger. Does the positive outweigh the negative, or visa versa? Go with your gut answer. The first answer is usually the right one for you in this moment. Listen to it. It's always talking to you. You just have to be willing to listen.

Again, negative means that these thoughts are harmful to you, positive means that they are beneficial to you and neutral means that there is no effect in your life at all when you have these thoughts. Write your conclusions on the table given on page 180 or in your journal.

    Mia stated that her thoughts were both positive and negative. She admitted that her thoughts were not as positive as she might have once thought, but that they must serve her in some way.

Step 5 Exercises

To find out which charge your thoughts are, fill in the following statements.

My thoughts benefit me because:

_____
_____
_____
_____

My thoughts hurt me because:

_____
_____
_____
_____

My thoughts don't affect me at all because:

_____
_____
_____
_____

Using the space below just write the word(s) Positive, Negative, and/or Neutral.

Charge(s) of Thoughts is/are

_____
_____

Step 6

Broken Record in Your Mind

"We are not at peace with others because we are not at peace with ourselves, and we are not at peace with ourselves because we are not at peace with God."

– Thomas Merton

When we start to identify our thoughts, we begin to see a pattern in them. This pattern has been a habitual behavior for many years, in fact, probably for most of our lives. Here we need to identify the unconscious repetitive statements in our mind that trigger our behavioral patterns. What we perpetually say to ourselves in our heads makes it a reality.

Look at an affirmation as a mantra. Very basically, a mantra is a sound or phrase that is meaningful to you and somehow connected with the universe. When you repeat it over and over again, it is meant to have a lot of power. This is exactly what you are doing on an unconscious level by incessantly repeating negative thoughts in your head. You are giving a phrase or belief a lot of power that may or may not be of any service to you anymore. But because it is unconscious, you can't do anything about it. If you are conscious of it then you can replace that thought with one that will benefit you instead of hurting you.

Let me explain. If I continuously think to myself (my negative, unconscious affirmation) that I am

uncomfortable and awkward in front of people and I fear
that circumstance, then I will only see how uncomfortable
and awkward I am in those circumstances. I am creating
that reality by my perception. Assume I am in a social
gathering and a person is speaking to me. I am listening,
but feeling uncomfortable and awkward. I respond to the
person already with the predisposition that I will make a
strange and awkward comment. While I am speaking,
the person notices something in the distance and makes
a strange face. Since I am hyper-sensitive to being judged
as awkward and uncomfortable, I assume that the person
is making a strange face because of me. Therefore, I will
spend the rest of the evening in a corner out of fear of
facing a situation like that again. Those social gatherings
will always control my life because I will avoid them at all
costs. I will find the awkwardness in any situation even
if I am not awkward.   I will see it in things that aren't
even happening – a deluded perception. I will interpret
my reality as that because I have habitually told myself
that for many years. It is a self-fulfilling prophecy and I
recognize this behavior and identify with it as who I am.

Identifying your thoughts helps you to begin to identify
your unconscious affirmation(s).   They are directly
connected. Affirmations can be positive, negative, or
neutral. A negative affirmation is any consistent phrase
in your mind that causes you constant pain and suffering
either on a physical, emotional, psychological, mental,
or energetic level. If you have chronic back pain and
you constantly say to yourself and others, "I have chronic
back pain," you will continuously feel chronic back pain.

Instead you could look at your chronic back pain and say to yourself something like, "I am healing my back." The word "pain" isn't involved and neither is the word "chronic." If you say you are healing your back, then you are allowing a different kind of mentality and energy to work through you. You have decided to change a negative, unconscious affirmation into a positive, conscious one.

Most of us will start with some negative affirmations because those are the ones that usually resonate the most and stand out more than the positive ones.

A positive affirmation is something that we say to ourselves constantly in order to feel better about ourselves and heal. Some ego might be involved in this kind of affirmation. When the ego is involved, most likely so is our level of attachment. This is why we identify the positive affirmation and then see if it will be helpful to change it into a neutral one. For example, I can think to myself, "I am the best teacher ever." In this phrase, I am using my ego to talk to myself. By thinking I am the best, then that must mean that there are other teachers who are worse than I am. This separates me from others and only ultimately makes me suffer although I may not notice it right now. Therefore, by identifying that I may think I am the best yoga teacher ever, I can change my affirmation to "I am who I am" or "I do my best as a teacher." As you can see, these last two affirmations are universal facts. They aren't opinions of myself of being good or bad, positive or negative. I am merely accepting the present circumstances as they are.

You have been using your Rolodex of negative

thoughts for the duration of your life so far. You have
been your own worst critique and knocked yourself down
long enough. This Rolodex hasn't worked for you thus
far; therefore, it is time to choose which new Rolodex of
positive and neutral thoughts will penetrate your mind
and change your perception of reality. This new way of
thinking will be revealed to you in Step 11: Change your
Mind.

Mia's negative affirmation was, "I am undesirable,
unlovable, unaccepted, and so different from everybody
else."

Step 6 Exercises

Unconscious Affirmations Exercise

Write down five to eight examples of unconscious negative affirmations that you say to yourself in relation to the behavior chosen.
You might need to do the meditation exercise here as well if you are having trouble.

1. _____

2. _____

3. _____

4. _____

5. _____

6. _____

7. _____

8. _____

My unconscious negative affirmation is

_____
_____
_____
_____
_____

Step 7

Whose Thoughts are These?

"Peace is to be found only within, and unless one finds it there he will never find it at all. Peace lies not in the external world. It lies within one's own soul."

– Ralph Waldo Trine

Where do your thoughts come from? Identifying the source of your thoughts is a pivotal step in your healing process. This might be your mom, dad, siblings, society, news, you, school, work, friends, etc. This step may be simpler than the other steps because we as humans tend to see how other people hurt us or hinder us. Many people feed off feeling like a victim of society and the circumstances of their lives. If you find yourself constantly complaining and feeling victimized, then I suggest you go back to your behavior pattern in Step 2 and add that in as well.

It's important not to place any blame on your source(s) during this process. We, as humans, easily attribute responsibility for our pain and actions to others, but the truth is that we are the only ones responsible for our actions, as you will continue to learn during this process. Remember to go deep. If you feel stuck in this step, keep asking yourself, "But where did that thought come from? And where did that thought come from?" until you get to the heart of it.

In Mia's example, her stream of consciousness was, "I'm

not sure why I withdraw from people... other than that is the way my family is and so it's what I learned growing up... we never shared our negative emotions... If we had problems we would just mind our own business... We wouldn't share... It was considered a weakness... And so I never connected with them deeply, only superficially... So indirectly I learned you can't trust people... you can't rely on others, they will always hurt you... that is what my family taught me... My source is also the past rejections which hurt my ego..."

We hold onto so much as humans. We are constantly dwelling in the past, and it is often difficult to get over that hump and bring ourselves into the present in order to move on. We all have several physical and emotional scars that don't allow us to move forward and realize the potential that we were destined to become. We are constantly bringing ourselves back to our unconscious habits, usually developed in childhood, time and time again. The only way to move forward is to identify these habits, where they came from, and why we are doing them. Then we can choose to either continue to live in habitual suffering, or become conscious and aware and choose to change for our best. We usually feel that we have to compromise ourselves for others, out of fear of what others might think. Remember that this process is only for you. This is your treat to yourself after years of unhealthily giving of your energy, body, mind, and emotions.

Imagine how your daily dynamic might change if you were consciously choosing where you were going, what you were saying, and how you were acting. You might say, "Well, I know I'm going to the grocery store today, and I'm going to work and I'm going to dinner, etc...," but that's not what I mean. What I mean is that every step of your life might just be you lost in thought about the pain and suffering you are in that is caused by your past. You don't even notice all the things around you that are happening like the beautiful, simple things. If each step, each thought, each word and each action you had was a bit more conscious then you might act differently.

For example, when we are driving and someone cuts us off, many of us tend to react, "Oh, f*$% you," and honk. We get so upset because some person is on their way to their destination and decided to cut us off. We have to remember that nothing is personal, so the fact that a complete stranger cut us off cannot possibly upset us. But it does, and in fact, it enrages us. Does this stranger know us? Did we do anything to this stranger that this stranger is unaware of? Are we secretly having an affair with the spouse of the stranger? I highly doubt it. Therefore, we need to remember to think consciously when confronted with difficult circumstances in order to maintain our own inner peace.

According to ancient yoga scriptures called the Yoga Sutras discovered by Patanjali, there are four keys to maintaining peace. The first key is to be friendly towards the happy. The second is to have compassion towards the unhappy. The third is to have reverence towards the holy, and the last is to have indifference towards those who act wickedly. If you can use the right key in any situation, then you are able to maintain your peace. The problem is that many people mix up the keys and add all sorts of their own variables. You will find many selfish people who are jealous of the happy, condescending or indifferent towards the unhappy, disrespectful of the holy, and friendly or reverent towards those acting wickedly. These people might be many things—hurt, confused, evil, lonely, etc. They will most likely find it hard to be happy, which is very unfortunate for them and everyone around them.

If we go back to the cutting-off-the-car example and we decide to be a bit more conscious, we might stop and say to ourselves, "It's ok. I'm not hurt. It's not that big a deal." But if we are already on edge and annoyed and frustrated with life, then, of course, we are going to honk back with all our might and maybe even hold down the horn for a good ten seconds just to piss the other person off. And then he gets pissed off and then you feel good: "Yeah, I showed him." But no, you didn't. That is a false sense of reality. All you've done is successfully made another person as annoyed as you are and maybe five other drivers around you that witnessed the whole thing. Then, you go home and tell the story to your family. Now they are pissed off too, cursing the random stranger on the street for something that might have happened three hours ago.

Do you see the chain of events? What was the source of your thoughts? How did you get to that point? You originally were suffering and unhappy with where you were right then and there. This caused a handful of other people to suffer and be unhappy as well. And maybe they caused someone else to suffer, and it goes on and on. This shows the influence you can have on your children or your family members too, so wouldn't you want to start teaching your children and family how to be happy and peaceful? You can only teach them once you know how to be happy and peaceful yourself.

So let's alleviate your suffering a bit and increase your happiness and peace a bit more so maybe you won't honk at the person next time but rather think twice. And when you think twice, that is consciousness. Act, instead of react. You are on the roadmap to peace and following the green flags. That means that you are applying the steps and the formula is working.

If you don't think twice and you still honk, but notice your reaction afterwards, it's ok. At least you noticed and that, too, is consciousness. Don't be too hard on yourself and just promise yourself to make some extra effort next time. Keep in mind that this process and healing is for you, so go at your own pace. And trust me, you will have plenty of chances to observe and control your reactions, especially in traffic.

Step 7 Exercises

My behavior is

_____

_____

_____

Thoughts leading to this behavior are

_____

_____

_____

Source Exercise 1

Early childhood relationships with the following sources in
relation to your behavior and thoughts:
You don't have to write them all out. Choose only the
sources that resonate with your behavior.

1. Mother

_____

_____

_____

2. Father

_____

_____

_____

3. Sibling(s)

_____

_____

_____

4. Grandparent(s)

_____

_____

_____

5. Elementary school friend(s):

_____

_____

_____

6. Elementary school teacher(s):

_____

_____

_____

7. High school friend(s):

_____

_____

_____

8. High school teacher(s):

_____

_____

_____

9. Society:

_____

_____

_____

10. Media, ie. magazines, TV, ads:

_____

_____

_____

Source Exercise 2

Present relationships with the following sources in relation to
your behavior and thoughts:
You don't have to write them all out. Choose only the
sources that resonate with your behavior.

1. Spouse/Significant Other:

_____
_____
_____

2. Children (if applicable):

_____
_____
_____

3. Mother

_____
_____
_____

4. Father

_____
_____
_____

5. Sibling(s)

_____
_____
_____

6. Grandparent(s)

_____
_____
_____

7. Employer(s) (if applicable):

_____
_____
_____

8. Colleague(s):

_____

_____

_____

9. College friend(s):

_____

_____

_____

10. College teacher(s):

_____

_____

_____

11. Society:

_____

_____

_____

12. Media, ie. magazines, TV, ads:

_____

_____

_____

The source(s) of my thoughts is/are

_____

_____

_____

_____

_____

_____

_____

Step 8

Effect of Thoughts

"The great teachings unanimously emphasize that all the peace, wisdom, and joy in the universe are already within us; we don't have to gain, develop, or attain them. We're like a child standing in a beautiful park with his eyes shut tight. We don't need to imagine trees, flowers, deer, birds, and sky; we merely need to open our eyes and realize what is already here, who we really are – as soon as we quit pretending we're small and unholy."

– Unknown

Some thoughts serve you and some don't. By identifying which ones serve you and which ones don't, you can begin to consciously shift your mind. So, at this point, you know your behavior, your thoughts and unconscious affirmations, the source of these thoughts and whether they are positive, negative, and/or neutral. Now we take it one step further and identify whether these thoughts are beneficial or harmful to you. Refrain from being judgmental and don't think of whether the thoughts are good or bad. It shouldn't be hard to identify this step. If your thoughts were identified as negative, then most likely they are harmful for you. If you identified them as positive thoughts, then they are beneficial.

Just be honest and truthful with yourself. If the thoughts are harmful, then you will want to be aware of this pattern in order to heal and eliminate it in a productive way. If you find that the thoughts are beneficial, then you can continue to use this pattern to your advantage and consciously choose to feel harmonious.

You are beginning to choose which thoughts you can

keep and which ones you can discard. You don't have to own your thoughts. Most of your thoughts were imposed on you anyway by parents, society, media, etc. so this is a great editing process.

So, now there is a clear decision here you have to make. The choice is yours. You can keep reading or stop now. This is where you make the choice of wanting to overcome this harmful behavior and take responsibility for your actions and life, or you can choose to sit back, let life continue to happen for you, and continue to suffer. You may not be ready for this process, and that is ok.

Mia identified her thoughts as harmful and she decided she was ready to keep going.

Your destiny and the universe are waiting for you to take responsibility for your life and to lead you to health and conscious living. It is what all of the great sages have talked about. The path to self-realization and self-discovery is a clear path that all souls must eventually take in order to heal and find peace, but you have to make the decision to do it in this life you have now. Who knows what the next moment will bring? You only have this moment to make a decision. If you make the choice to continue, you will have to remember that you will have moments when you are frustrated with this process and will want to stop. So, stop if you want to and come back to it when you feel more inspired. Be patient with yourself. Know that everyone is feeling just as frustrated as you. If you do stop for a bit, know that you will come back to it eventually, so it is in your best interest to keep working slowly toward healing and peace. This process could take a while, in fact, most people spend their whole lives working towards finding peace, but not knowing how to do it.

Here is your map to start clearly and take it moment by moment. Don't get obsessed with needing to finish. In fact, you could never finish. You could be tricking yourself into thinking you are done, but you could be staying superficial with your answers. Go a bit deeper until something inside you says, "Oh, wow, that's where it is. That's what Rina has been talking about." You will know, unless you lie to yourself and don't listen to your gut, which is an easy habit to form when dealing with issues that you don't want to face.

Listening to your intuition is a habit that you will want to cultivate on a daily basis. Do it at least once a day or, if that is too intense for you now, once a week. But make clear the distinction between listening to your gut versus listening to your mind. Listening to your gut is very closely related to listening to your heart. Experience the difference within yourself so that you can easily distinguish it. You could be lost in an emotion and not listen to the lower voice, your gut or intuition that speaks from deep down inside your body. This will serve as a very important tool for the rest of your life. If you are already in tune with listening to your gut then use it during this process. In fact, you have already started practicing this skill in the meditation exercises given to you earlier in the book.

So, if you want to stop with the steps now, listen to your gut and see what it says. If it says to stop, then stop. If it says to keep going, then keep going. Remember, your gut is not your mind, which is usually associated with your ego. Your ego is a powerful thing that blocks you from deeper spiritual growth and hinders you as a soul. It only seems to elevate your identification with your body, your name, your possessions, your popularity, your money, your power, and your false sense of self.

Be your own detective and figure yourself out. If you are moving on, keep reading. If you are pausing, then I would like to say thank you and I hope to see you again soon.

Step 8 Exercises

Listening to your Gut Exercise

Similar to the meditation exercise previously given, you could sit comfortably in a quiet place.

This time, instead of writing down your thoughts as they come up, I want you to categorize your thoughts as they surface. Whatever thoughts come up I want you to distinguish whether your mind, your heart or your gut is talking to you. Thoughts associated with your mind will want to judge, criticize, belittle, or gloat and keep you connected with the external world. They will also keep you in the past or in the future, most likely worried about either one. Plus, they are thoughts that are logical and rational. Thoughts associated with your heart will evoke feelings and emotions, positive and negative. There is no logic with thoughts associated with your heart. And lastly, thoughts associated with your gut will usually be connected to your intuition or instinct, which tells you some sort of truth in the present moment. Unfortunately, these thoughts usually get drowned out by a thought associated with your mind. Thought associated with your gut or intuitions are a lot quieter. You have to be paying special attention to those by making the thoughts in the mind quieter.

Sit for about 10 minutes doing this exercise. Count how many times you have a thought in each category.

Thoughts associated with your mind:

_____
_____
_____

Thoughts associated with your heart:

_____
_____
_____

Thoughts associated with your gut:

_____
_____
_____

Am I Ready? Exercise

After doing the previous exercise, ask yourself if you are ready to continue on this journey right now.

If not, you may want to return to it at a later date. You can sit quietly and see which part of you is answering when you ask this question.

Am I ready to continue? My mind says_____

Am I ready to continue? My heart says_____

Am I ready to continue? My gut says _____

If you feel you are ready, this means that you are prepared to take responsibility for every action and situation you have been in and any decision you have made. You are empowering yourself because you have decided that you will not be a victim to others even if they have been hurtful towards you.

This will be more clearly explained in the chapters to come.

Are you ready? Circle one.

- Yes -

- No -

- Don't Know -

Are the effects of your thoughts beneficial or harmful?

_____
_____
_____

Step 9

It's a Vicious Cycle

"If we are to teach real peace in this world, and if we are to carry on a real war against war, we shall have to begin with the children."

– Mahatma Gandhi

Identifying your belief systems might be tricky and painful at first. For the purposes of this book, a belief system does not have a religion connotation but instead is a series of conditioned thoughts and actions mastered by you, motivated by an unconscious fear that is usually generated at an early age. You created the system by convincing yourself it was necessary in order to cope with whatever circumstance was given to you. In other words, you designed a behavior or pattern that allowed you to protect yourself and survive in this world, driven by a deep-rooted belief created in early childhood.

One of Mia's belief systems was "Because of my fear of feeling rejected, hurt and unloved, I put up walls and refrained from allowing anyone into my heart and world in order to prevent myself from further pain and suffering. Better to not let people into my life and pretend everything is ok, than for them to know how hurt I really am. This way they don't have any power over me." She came up with this because as a child she was very loving and tried to reach out to her parents and family by being herself and being open, but she didn't receive the same treatment in return. She unfortunately learned early on that she shouldn't act this way or the world (parents) would respond negatively towards her. Therefore, she created this belief system in order to protect herself from further pain and suffering in this world. She unconsciously figured that if she blocked people out and denied being herself, she could blend in and be accepted into society. This, of course, was not all figured out when she was a child, so she has been reacting unconsciously in this way for most of her existence.

Another example could be someone who identifies his problematic action as "drinking too much." After much soul searching, one individual realized that the reason he felt he had to drink was in order to be accepted in society and know how to relate to others. When he searched deeper, he discovered that he had started drinking so that he wouldn't feel awkward in society and be rejected. Therefore, his belief system might have started at age 17 when he didn't want to get his feelings hurt. He feared rejection; therefore, he created the belief system that if he drank alcohol people would accept him. He then discovered that he didn't only use alcohol to protect his feelings. Before alcohol, he had smoked cigarettes and marijuana starting at age 12, and before that he overate, which started in early childhood. So he always used something in order to feel accepted by society. He used these substances as a way to not get his feelings hurt and to prevent the feeling of rejection. These belief systems are our defense mechanisms we create and live with because we do not want to cope with our hurt feelings.

In order to begin the healing process you must discover the detrimental belief system that has been with you for the majority of your life. When you discover this, you will see how much power this pattern has had over your whole life. At this point, it will be easy for some of you to become depressed and to feel that you have wasted your whole life with an attachment to this pattern. If you do tend to get depressed often then you might consider going through the 15-Step process for that behavior if it overwhelms you. Observe the fact that you might feel like that in a moment, but don't attach to it. As one of my teachers always says, "Allow things to appear and disappear."

Be positive and realize that you finally have begun to solve the puzzle of your life, which is one of the most empowering moments you will experience. Now you can move through life with awareness of your tendencies and begin to shift and change them each moment they arise. You want this to become your daily habit. You want this to become your new pattern. You must brainwash yourself, clean yourself of all your dirty, messy, harmful thoughts and replace them with conscious, pure, and healthy ones. (We will learn how to create these healthy thoughts in Step 11.) Notice I didn't say good thoughts. What are good thoughts? They are relative to each person, correct? Which leads us to the next step. But first, the exercises for this step.

Step 9 Exercises

Fear Exercise

Take a moment to think about your fears. Use the spaces below to help you direct your thoughts. Please use your journal in order to write your stream of consciousness regarding each statement. Use this exercise with as many of your fears as you want.

Recall your behavior. With your behavior in mind, fill in the blanks below.

I have a fear of

_____

_____

_____

I have a fear of feeling

_____

_____

_____

I have this fear because

_____

_____

_____

My first memory of feeling this fear was

_____

_____

_____

My reaction to feeling this fear was

_____

_____

_____

The way I react now when I feel this fear is

_____

_____

Do I want to overcome this fear? Why or Why not?

_____

_____

_____

Belief System(s) Exercise

Once you have discovered your belief system, test it and see if it reigns true. For example, Mia thinks she is unattractive and undesirable. Therefore, when she is in a social gathering and she is feeling undesirable, her negative affirmation pops into her head, and she recalls her belief system. Since she is able to identify it and observe it in that moment, she has the choice to keep using it or change it. She decides to consciously change that conditioned behavior of slouching, feeling ugly, and hiding in the corner by doing something new. The new behavior was to smile at someone who is smiling at her. If the person decides to start a conversation, she vows to not walk away but be more open.

Remember to be aware of the self-fulfilling prophecy we discussed earlier in the book.

To help you find your belief system creating your behavior, in your journal, you are going to write down the details of a situation you are typically in.

Write down the following:

Recall a specific or general date: _____

Typical event/situation:

_____

_____

_____

Your usual reaction/behavior:

_____

_____

_____

Your feelings after this usual reaction/behavior:

_____

_____

_____

What new behavior might be helpful:

_____

_____

_____

Desired effects of using new behavior:

_____

_____

_____

Now write down an actual situation that has happened to you after reading this step. You will need to come back to this one.

Date: _____

Actual event/situation:

_____

_____

_____

Your usual reaction/behavior:

_____

_____

_____

Your feelings after this usual reaction/behavior:

_____

_____

_____

Ability to observe yourself using this behavior:

_____

_____

_____

Choice of new conscious behavior:

_____

_____

_____

Attempted new conscious behavior:

_____

_____

_____

Ability to observe yourself using new behavior:

_____

_____

_____

Effects of using new behavior:

_____

_____

_____

Could you maintain a bit more peace using this new behavior? Why or why not?

_____

_____

_____

My belief system in relation to my behavior is

_____

_____

_____

Step 10

What is Truth?

"Everything is changeable, everything appears and disappears; there is no blissful peace until one passes beyond the agony of life and death."

– Buddha

Discover the difference between your relative truths and the absolute truths of the universe.

Discover the relative truth behind the belief system you noted in the previous step. The truth is that all your behaviors, thoughts, and beliefs in the past were based on your relative truth in that moment. Relative truth is similar to saying your own personal truth. You used your defense mechanisms and ego in order to protect yourself from the world you lived in. Whether right or wrong, it doesn't matter. What matters is that you are here now and want to heal. You needed those defense mechanisms and your belief system at that time in your life and chose them out of fear. This is what everyone does, and it is completely normal and understandable. We have all done that. But that was needed in the past, not now. You are a more conscious person now and have chosen to take your life into your hands and look for lasting peace.

I don't think that the universe would place all these humans on earth just to make them suffer endlessly. If there is a yin, there is a yang. So if you are constantly suffering, know that there is a way to constantly be in peace. Just like it takes work to suffer though, it takes work to find peace. It's not just something that accidentally hits you in the head. It's something that, when you are ready to listen, will hit you in one moment by a feeling of, "Aha! I feel it!" You can't force it. But you must prepare yourself to be ready by doing these steps and exercises.

If you want to become an Olympic champion, you don't just wait until the day before the games begin and expect to be strong enough, flexible enough, and in the best shape of your life in order to win the gold. You have to work at it. If you speak to an Olympian, he/she will tell you about practicing for hours and hours with no end in sight. He/she has to constantly be practicing.

It is the same for this process. Just as in the Belief System Exercise, you must start to catch yourself in moments when you are unconscious and being reactive. It is a treacherous and never-ending journey, but it is worthwhile. It gets easier. Everyone eventually gets those "aha!" moments of realization. The Olympic gold for us is the moment-to-moment conscious awareness and choosing to maintain our inner peace. If you set yourself up to have a goal and a timeline, then you will fail because you will get disappointed. I can guarantee you that, and I am speaking from my own experience. But maybe you have to set those goals and expectations, in order for you to fall several times and finally get back up and say, "Wait a minute. This isn't working for me anymore. What am I doing wrong?"

That past relative truth motivated by your belief system is no longer yours to own. The "child you" needed it because you didn't know about choices, but the older you is more aware and is more willing to choose and to take responsibility for your actions.

Explore the difference between the relative truth you live and the absolute truth of the universe. The relative truth includes your likes, dislikes, opinions, views, your feelings, and how you perceive things around you in certain moments. One sequence of events will have several different versions and perceptions of the truth depending on who you ask. So then what is the truth? The relative truth is different for each party involved or each person telling the story. Each person adds his/her own beliefs, twists, excitement, emotions, judgments, and opinions, which have all been based on the belief systems and relative truths learned in the past.

Relative truth is true at only one time and at one place. It's true to some people and not to others. It's true now but it may not have been true in the past, or vise versa. It also may not be true in the future because it is always subject to change and subject to the perspectives of people.

For example, imagine a man and a woman who have been married for several years. The woman is self-conscious about her weight and the man tends to be a bit insensitive at times. The man and woman are getting ready for a birthday party for one of their friends' kids at a park. The woman walks out of the bedroom wearing all black and tells her husband she's ready. He reacts to her outfit by saying, "You are going to wear that?" She gets upset because she thinks he is calling her fat and ugly, based on her insecurities. She runs back to the bedroom upset, and her husband is confused about what he said. His concern was that she was going to wear all black to a kid's birthday party during the day. She would probably be uncomfortable, overdressed, and hot. The woman's perception was that her husband was being insensitive and mean. He approaches her, but she is mad. Since she won't talk to him, he gets upset also. They go to the party, but they remain mad at each other and they don't enjoy what could have been a festive and happy moment.

This basic example shows us how a simple misunderstanding based on relative truths for each person creates a problem and destroys inner peace.

This happens all the time. Let me repeat that: This happens all the time.

The facts of the story were the following:
Man and woman are going to a kid's birthday party at a park.
Woman decides to wear black to party.
Man asks question.
Woman gets upset.
Man gets upset.
Day is ruined for man and woman.

Those are the facts. The rest of the story is based on the perceptions of each person. I'm sure if you asked the woman and the man separately what happened, they would give you two totally different stories. And that is relative truth.

Absolute truth applies to everyone and is not specific to one person. Because this truth applies to everyone at all times and in all places, it is called absolute. These are the laws and truths of the universe. Whether you believe in absolute truth or not doesn't matter because it applies to you anyway. It applies at all times, in all places, to all beings. It cannot be invented or created by man like relative truth can be. Instead, it is truth that can be discovered and realized.

Some absolute truths of the universe include the laws of karma, the laws of gravity, and the quantum physics principle that we are all made of energy particles. In addition, there is the cycle of life, which includes the principles of creation, preservation, destruction, or life, death, and transformation (rebirth.) Some more examples include the following: we all are born, we all die, we need food and water to survive, we need air to breathe, our bodies get older and decay with age, gravity applies to everyone, everything is constantly changing, and you cannot have two mountains without a valley in between.

Because everything in life is created, preserved, and destroyed, everything is impermanent. Look at any business, project, person, sound, relationship, government, family, idea, feeling, emotion, thought, etc. It never stays the same. Everything is constantly changing. We can hold onto ideas and thoughts, like our belief systems, from our past to feel that things are permanent. This tends to bring us some temporary deluded comfort, but in fact, it will cause more stress than comfort in the long run. This is because we are resisting the natural flow of change that exists in the universe. Moving with change allows us to be open and to discover things that otherwise would never be discovered. Attachment is the main reason we suffer. We want so badly to believe that we control the things around us and that we have ultimate control over our lives. Unfortunately, we don't have any control over what happens to us. We only have control over how we act and think.

There is a truth that I have chosen to believe as an absolute truth, but I have no evidence of it, just faith and what I have learned from my experiences with yoga. I invite you to apply this method of thinking as it will help you understand yourself a lot more. Regardless of whether it is absolute or relative, it works and is very powerful. The truth I refer to includes the idea that we as energy entities contain two influential and intelligent sides: the ego and the pure self.

The ego, which we all know too well, identifies with every label such as man, woman, doctor, mother, teacher, daughter, father, rich, poor, handsome, ugly, etc. The ego usually feels superior or inferior to someone or something else at any given time. It is imperative to start to look at which thoughts are driven by the ego. Do you feel that you are better than or worse than someone in any moment? These thoughts are driven by the idea of duality. For example, "I am a good mother" implies that there must be three other external entities dependent on that thought to compare to. One: A child must be born so that there can be a mother. Two: The concept of man because a mother implies a woman. Three: The concept of what is bad and what is good.

Since we were born, we have been shown comparison

after comparison. Our mind has been programmed to compare, analyze, and judge. In fact, that is the nature of the mind: to judge. Therefore, we want to observe this judgment if it arises because doing so will automatically take us to a place of truth.

This place of truth, the pure self, is the other side of us. It is a lot quieter since it is egoless and non-dual in nature. This pure self is the one that we are connecting to throughout the process of this book. This place is where our inner peace lies. But, we have to start accessing it by listening more earnestly. The pure self will never be completely deleted from us, but we have to use it in order to strengthen it and make it louder. If we use the ego side of ourselves too much, we know where that takes us: to suffering by a heightened or diminished false sense of self. Most of the time we are stuck in the ego world where we either feel better than or worse than someone or something else, which in my experience feels really crummy. So, if we are 85 percent in this ego side and only 15 percent in the pure self, then we will want to take conscious steps towards the pure self. And, I have good news for you. Just by consciously choosing to heal yourself as you are right now by reading this book, you are in the pure self. So congrats! But, watch your thoughts! If you automatically felt a sense of grandeur and a need to gloat, then you transferred yourself into the ego self. The ego is tricky. It creeps up on you. Develop a watchful eye and gain keen awareness. I guarantee that you will start to feel better even if at first you are shocked as to how many things you had hidden in your thoughts and mind. Just be aware, don't judge what arises.

As we become more aware, things present themselves in ways that we had been oblivious to before. For a simple example, when you buy a new car, you notice that model of car is now everywhere on the road. Before, you didn't notice it, but now it seems that everyone has bought the same car as you. What's actually happened is that you are now more aware of it than before. The cars were already there, but because your energy and consciousness has shifted to that car, now you are open to seeing it on the road. Before you were closed off to it and didn't care. It didn't affect you either way. But now, it has a whole new meaning to you.

This step is obviously one that takes contemplation and time. This will not be an overnight "Aha!" realization. I urge you to analyze and think deeply about the difference between relative truth and absolute truth. Research it on the Internet or buying some of my recommended books to help you understand this idea further. Observe how absolute truths apply to everyone, but how your relative truths only apply to you. Not everyone likes and does the things you like and do, and vice versa.

At this point, you can read on even if you haven't understood or felt the difference between relative truth and absolute truth. But just keep in mind that you might need to pause in whichever step you feel you haven't realized or discovered. Don't jump ahead in your own process, but you might want to read the last few steps as a way to give you a heads-up of what's coming. But, it's up to you.

Step 10 Exercises

Relative Truth Experiment

Do a little experiment. Tell a few people the same story. Then ask each person to answer a few questions about the story. Come up with your own questions. See what each one of them gets from that story.

Then ask them to retell the story back to you or to someone else. See how they modify it or add to it.

It's imperative that you don't judge them or yourself in the process. If you find yourself in constant judgment by thinking that something is good and something is bad, then I urge you to do the 15 Steps with "being judgmental" as your behavior for Step 2. It will reveal a lot for you. But, finish this behavior first.

Third Person Exercise

In this step, you will refer to yourself in the third person. It is highly beneficial for you to do this because you are able to separate yourself emotionally and observe your life from a distance.

Take a moment to think of a story that happened to you recently. Tell the story aloud as if you were telling it to a friend. Then, tell the story again, but replace the word "I" with your name. You will probably catch yourself a few times saying "I." Now, restate the sentence using your name. If you feel foolish speaking aloud to yourself, merely write the story down in your journal. Please be aware that you will most likely not do this exercise with other people because you might feel more outcasted and only worsen the feeling of rejection. Do this exercise on your own or with a true friend who is going to understand or is going through a similar process. Speaking about yourself in the third person is not something that all people will understand or support, so be selective as to whom you discuss your healing process with. If you wrote the story in your journal, then you can read it aloud.

When you are done, notice the effect this exercise had on you, if any. Write down the effect:

_____

_____

How did you feel speaking in the third person?

_____

_____

_____

How did others feel when you spoke about yourself in the third person? Did they understand?

_____

_____

_____

How many times did you say the word "I" or "me?"

_____

_____

_____

How many times did you catch yourself and say your name?

_____

_____

_____

Who's Talking? Ego vs. Pure Self Exercise 1

Please identify whether you believe the following phrases or thoughts are spoken from your ego or pure self. Basically, answer the question, "Who's talking?" Spoken phrases are in quotation marks and thoughts are not. This is a very general exercise, but can be very effective in categorizing your thoughts and intentions. This exercise can be tricky, so listen to the voice behind the sentences to feel the intention and the source of those words and statements. Support each answer with an explanation as to why you chose what you chose.

1. I showed him. "I'm sorry if it didn't turn out as you planned."

_____

_____

_____

2. She looks great in that dress. "You look great."

_____

_____

_____

3. I feel fat.

_____

_____

_____

4. I can't believe she is going to make me pay again. "Sure, I'll pay. Don't worry."

_____

_____

_____

5. I'm alive.

_____

_____

_____

6. "Do you need me to help? I'm available."

_____

_____

_____

7. How can I pay those bills? "I don't have enough money."

_____

_____

_____

8. The rain feels moist.

_____
_____
_____

9. "I love you, but why can't this be like this?"

_____
_____
_____

10. I love myself.

_____
_____
_____

Some answers for the above exercise, could be, but are not limited to, the following:
1.   Ego.
2.   Pure Self.
3.   Ego.
4.   Ego.
5.   Pure Self.
6.   Pure Self.
7.   Ego.
8.   Pure Self.
9.   Ego.
10.   Pure Self.

Please take a moment to compare your notes. You can debate either way. Please make our opinion understood so that it is clear that you understand.

Who's Talking? Ego vs. Pure Self Exercise 2

Now, using your thoughts and words from Steps 4, 6, and 7, answer the question, "Who's talking?" Listen to who is really talking. Remember to be aware of your intention behind your statements.

1. _____
_____
_____

2. _____
_____
_____

3. _____
_____
_____

4. _____
_____
_____

Write out your ideas on relative truth vs. absolute truth.
Use your journal if you need more space.

_____
_____
_____
_____
_____
_____
_____
_____

Step 11

Change Your Mind

"Peace is a daily, a weekly, a monthly process, gradually changing opinions, slowly eroding old barriers, quietly building new structures."

– John Fitzgerald Kennedy

In Step 6, "Broken Record in Your Mind," I discuss how to start changing your unconscious negative affirmation into a positive one. For example, if I usually say to myself that I feel awkward and uncomfortable in social settings, then I might start saying instead "I am relaxed and comfortable," when in those situations. Use positive affirmations when you notice your mind going off into your habitual, delusional, repetitive "comfort zone." Start changing negative affirmations to positive ones.

These affirmations could change how you feel about yourself. As I mentioned before, you have a broken record in your mind of the same detrimental thoughts you've had since you were a child, which have manifested themselves into your reality. So, now you are stopping that broken record and creating a new repetitive statement that helps you change your reality to how you want it. It only starts with changing the thoughts, but you can't stop there. You have to have your actions mirror your thoughts; otherwise you are remaining passive, and I guarantee you that you won't see favorable results.

Here are some examples of conscious positive

affirmations that you could apply: I am healthy. I am happy. I am conscious. I am considerate. I am giving. I am balanced. I am thoughtful. I am deserving. I am worthy. I am loved. I am safe. I am protected. I am comfortable. I am relaxed. I am focused. I am peaceful. I am trusting. I am accepted. I am loving. I am open. I am beautiful. I am able to express myself freely. I am perfect the way that I am.

These new phrases could all become part of your new Rolodex of thoughts and realities. Feel free to add to any of these or create your own. This is for you only. Plus, you will need to repeat these new phrases constantly in order to dilute the power of the old negative phrases. When I first started this form of healing, I would repeat the affirmations all the time even when I didn't think I needed them. I'd repeat them in the car, in the bathroom, as I was falling asleep, while I was eating, etc. I needed to wash my brain from the previous junk it had attached itself to unconsciously and start putting in the thought patterns that would benefit me the most. I allowed my mind to only become consumed with this new thought and paid attention to when the mind would want to pull itself towards a habitual form of thinking, which was of course, usually negative.

You will have your own unconscious negative affirmation. So, according to that affirmation, you can then choose the appropriate conscious positive one.

Mia chose the positive affirmation "I love and accept myself therefore I welcome others into my life."

Step 11 Exercises

Affirmation Exercise

Change the following negative affirmations to positive ones. Don't just add the word not to the statement. The whole sentence needs to be changed in order for it to be effective.

1. <u>Negative Affirmation</u>: I am less than worthy. I don't deserve this. <u>Positive Affirmation</u>:

_____

_____

_____

2. <u>Negative Affirmation</u>: I am alone and don't want to end up like my mother. <u>Positive Affirmation</u>:

_____

_____

_____

3. <u>Negative Affirmation</u>: I am always in the way. I am a burden. <u>Positive Affirmation</u>:

_____

_____

_____

4. <u>Negative Affirmation</u>: I am fat and ugly. I am not good enough. <u>Positive Affirmation</u>:

_____

_____

_____

5. <u>Negative Affirmation</u>: I am awkward and uncomfortable with others. <u>Positive Affirmation</u>:

_____

_____

_____

6. <u>Negative Affirmation</u>: I can handle everything. I
don't need anyone. <u>Positive Affirmation</u>:

_____

_____

_____

   Some possible ways to change the first two negative
affirmations above are, "I am deserving and worthy," and "I
follow my own path, and I am my own person." For affirmation
three, it could state, "I am useful and important to others." For
the fourth affirmation, "I am beautiful, lovable, and worthy."
For the fifth, "I embrace my surroundings and am comfortable
in all settings." For the last affirmation, one could say, "I accept
others' opinions and can grow from learning from others."
Figure out more options on your own. Remember to refrain
from using any negative words such as not, enough, and no.
   Make the affirmation personal to your behavior as well.

My unconscious negative affirmation was

_____

_____

_____

My new conscious positive affirmation is

_____

_____

_____

Step 12

Forgive Yourself

"For everything there is a season,
And a time for every matter under heaven:
A time to be born, and a time to die;
A time to plant, and a time to
pluck up what is planted;
A time to kill, and a time to heal;
A time to break down, and a time to build up;
A time to weep, and a time to laugh;
A time to mourn, and a time to dance;
A time to throw away stones,
and a time to gather stones together;
A time to embrace, and a time
to refrain from embracing;
A time to seek, and a time to lose;
A time to keep, and a time to throw away;
A time to tear and a time to sew;
A time to keep silence, and a time to speak;
A time to love, and a time to hate;
A time for war, and a time for peace."

– Ecclesiastes 3:1-8

Once you have discovered all of this truth about yourself, it is time to forgive yourself and find compassion for yourself, especially the "child you." Forgiving yourself is the same as accepting yourself. This is very hard because, from the time we are children, we are told we are wrong and we have to change our nature in order to conform to society. Our natural selves and emotions have been pushed down and repressed so much that it is very hard to find forgiveness or acceptance for ourselves. Our society is filled with self-blame and self-destruction, but as we tend to feel intuitively, this is harmful to us.

It is important to be able to forgive yourself; in fact, what you are forgiving and accepting is your story. This means that you have to start implementing all of the information you have learned about yourself in Steps 1 through 11. If not, all this valuable information stays cognitive and conceptual, and you won't be able to put it into practice. Forgiveness and compassion are vital because you cannot forgive or have compassion for others if you don't find it for yourself first. Thus, you cannot accept others as they are until you accept yourself as you are. This is when you realize, "Gosh, darn it, I did all those things in the past as reactions to the world around me, and I didn't have any control over them. It was completely an unconscious process based on protection and not on truth. Now that I am beginning to become more aware, I can choose my outcome and my actions. I can act, instead of react."

Reaction implies lack of awareness and being lost in a situation or emotion, while action implies being conscious of the effects your behaviors have on you and others. So, if you can truly realize that your past behaviors were based on reactions, then you can hopefully forgive yourself, because you didn't know any better. But now you do!

So it is time to act with more awareness of the effects of your behaviors and thoughts. Through the previous steps, you have been able to detect how a behavior, preceded by a thought and an unconscious affirmation, preceded by a belief system based on your environment as a child, has brought you to this moment. Next time you are confronted with a similar situation you are now going to be able to choose to use this method in order to guide yourself towards peace. But, search inwards to find this forgiveness and compassion. See that your past reactions were based on protection and relative truth and not on absolute truth and consciousness. You don't need to protect yourself anymore. You can start to learn how to transform learned, conditioned, reactionary behaviors into conscious, healthy, harmonious ones.

I personally experienced this step one day while I was sitting quietly at home. I remember I was contemplating many things, including my past mistakes, and it just hit me. I literally moved my head slightly back in awe as I clearly saw my past as Rina's story. Rina was experiencing the pain of her story, but now I had the choice to continue this way or make it my own, new story based on truth and conscious actions. It is something that I feel will just come to you when you are ready. It cannot be forced, but you can prepare yourself for when it does come and start heading in that general direction. The exercises on Forgiving Yourself are steps I took in this path towards forgiving myself.

Step 12 Exercises

Memory Exercise

You will need to bring up some tough memories from your past so be aware and ready for having some time to yourself.

Sit comfortably, either on the floor or in a chair in a quiet room alone.

You can choose to write in your journal or just contemplate.

Take a few deep breaths before you start.

Go through each memory from your past and think of every single person to whom you did some kind of harm. Only do one person at a time. Don't group people together. Individualize the process and personalize it. This will only help you heal further.

In your mind or on your paper, recall each person's name, your age at the time, the situation as best as you can, and what you did to each person exactly. Even if someone didn't know you did something to them, you will need to apologize to them.

Visualize the person in front of you and genuinely apologize for hurting their feelings or for whatever it is you did. Speak to them mentally from a place in your heart. Don't just mumble, "Sorry." Finish the sentence, "I apologize for _____."

Think and speak clearly. Remember, no one is judging you for this. Just be clear and heartfelt. You can even visualize the person forgiving you if you want. If you can't be heartfelt yet, then just write the list of people for now, knowing you will need to do this exercise again at a later date.

There will also be some people that you might want to verbally apologize to face-to-face. But, this is not necessary. This process is not for them; it's for you. You will know which people you need to express your feelings to. Be careful when drudging up the past for people. Not everyone is willing to feel these feelings with you. Be sensitive to others' personal paths and places in life. Use your intuition and gut to guide you as much as possible. If it seems difficult then maybe refrain from telling the person verbally. Again, it is not necessary to apologize in person. This healing is for you and if you can end up forgiving your past story then it may be irrelevant that the other person knows you are sorry.

Memory 1

Your approximate age:_____

Name of other person:_____

Situation:

_____

_____

_____

Action you are apologizing for:

_____

_____

_____

Inner effect of apologizing:

_____

_____

_____

Memory 2

Your approximate age:_____

Name of other person:_____

Situation:

_____

_____

_____

Action you are apologizing for:

_____

_____

_____

Inner effect of apologizing:

_____

_____

_____

Personal Definition and Experience of Compassion Exercise

What is your definition of compassion?

_____

_____

_____

Recall a time when you felt sincere compassion for another:

_____

_____

_____

Acceptance Exercise

Choose one thing you have never wanted to accept yourself for. I do not accept myself for

_____

_____

_____

Choose one thing you have always accepted about yourself. I have always accept myself for

_____

_____

_____

Step 13

Nothing is Personal

*"If you wish to experience peace,
provide peace for another."*

– Tenzin Gyatso, The 14th Dalai Lama

Discover that everyone else's actions are also based on their relative truths and see how their belief systems may have brought them to react a certain way in life and towards you. Therefore, how a person acts towards you is never personal. It is his/her own story.

Once you have realized all of your own personal truths and forgiven yourself, then you can begin to think of other people. Everyone has their own personal belief systems that cause him/her to protect him/herself in this world. A person's belief system is influenced by their surroundings and family, which lead them to think certain thoughts, triggering them to react the way they do. It's the same process for everyone. No one is singled out. We are all suffering with the same dilemmas together. But just as we are all the same in that we have all experienced our own relative truths, so it is that we can all heal ourselves. Again, I am reminding you that the yin (positive) and the yang (negative) elements are always needed. If we can get ourselves into this mess, we can get ourselves out. We just need some guidance because we have been lost for so long.

When you can identify that other people are also suffering and discover that they have created a pattern of reacting as you have, then you can begin to put yourself in their shoes and understand a bit more why people act the way they do. With awareness and understanding of yourself and others, comes peace, compassion, and acceptance of yourself and of others.

If you truly have been able to forgive yourself and your story, then this step will be easier for you. If you are feeling moments of blame and victimization, then you have not completely discovered the difference between the true you (absolute truth) and your story (relative truth.) Revisit them if you need to and remember that it's a process of ups and downs. Search a bit more for your truth. I cannot give you your truth; I can only guide you in the general direction that helped me heal my wounds and patterns. I had to suffer and fall many times to finally understand my folly. And I expect to fall and rise again many times more. I have learned to accept this as part of the process and I hope you will too. It will only bring you more peace.

Let me explain what I mean by "the way that people react towards you is never personal." Assume I am in a crappy mood one day because I am in one of my habitual behaviors, which means I am being reactive and not consciously acting, and someone says a nasty comment to me at the supermarket because I am blocking their shopping cart. Most likely, I will react to their perceiving "obvious" assault since I am stuck in my relative truth. I begin to react emotionally and talk back to the person "defending myself" from this "horrible, mean person." I say nasty things back to them and attack them back. Now, there are two people reacting to each other who have never met before. Is it really personal that this stranger said something nasty to me? Maybe this stranger has his or her own story, which could include the fact that they were taught by their parents to complain and whine when they want something. They, too, were "reacting" just like I was and just like most everyone else does in the world. But, I decided to take this person's story as a personal assault on me because I was protecting my belief system and my relative truth, "How dare this person attack me? Who do they think they are?"

We react with our ego. As we discussed before, ego is everyone's relative truth, which makes us feel that we are better than or worse than something or someone else. It's what separates us and makes us identify with external circumstances. Everyone's pure and truest self is absolute truth. If you can start to identify when you communicate with your ego then you will see how many times a day people speak with their egos. Most of their day is spent in ego form, in their heads, closed off and taking everything personally.

We trick ourselves into thinking that this is the "right" way because we have not been taught any other way, and we fear questioning what we have learned. Our society is made up of individuals. These individuals have all placed belief systems on themselves when they were just little children in order to protect themselves from what they perceived as the "big, bad, ugly world." What were they protecting themselves from? Mostly from fear of rejection, not being loved, getting their feelings hurt, and not being accepted as they truly are. Sound familiar?

Let's talk a little bit about karma. Karma literally means action. What it generally means is that to every action there is a reaction. But, it's not as simple as having bad or good karma as the term has commonly been used. According to the Yoga Sutras of Patanjali, there are actually three different kinds of karma. The first karma is the one you came into this life with. For example, the fact that you are born into this body already means that you have karma -past impressions- that you have to burn or cleanse from previous lives. The second karma is the karma that you are burning right now. This means that you are presently living the karma that you need to burn in this moment. So, whatever is happening to you in this moment is the process of your karma burning. And the third, which for me is the most important, is the karma that you are creating right now. This karma is the one we can change according to our actions and intentions in this very moment. So, to sum up, you have the stored karma that still has not been used up, the karma that you are burning now, and the karma that you are creating right now. The karma you are burning and creating can happen simultaneously because while a situation is "happening to you," you are either reacting unconsciously or acting consciously as a response, which can create more karma. I put "happening to you" in quotation marks because if we adopt these three karmas, then nothing is happening to you but happening because of you. You are responsible for everything that happens around you, therefore there is nothing to feel victimized about, especially when someone else is acting out and seeming to attack you. This person is choosing to act this way whether it's unconscious or not. It doesn't matter what you are doing. How you react to this person's actions and how you choose to feel about him/her is up to you. The other person also has to live by these laws of karma, so they have a choice as well. Unfortunately most of us don't think we have such choices or power in our lives. How someone chooses to react or feel about a situation is up to them and it is never personal. It's a decision they have made unconsciously based on their karma and past experiences. I hope you can see how this all correlates. It's very important to take this into consideration while you are processing so that you can start having complete awareness behind your decisions and choices. It's imperative that you take complete responsibility for everything that happens "to you."

Let me give you an example that I experienced of the three karmas so that you can get a better picture of how they are related.

Since I own a yoga studio and sell retail, I had a luggage of the retail clothing in the back seat of my car. I parked my car in the outside parking lot of my boyfriend's apartment complex and locked the door. I looked at the luggage and thought to myself "I should probably put in the trunk so it's not visible and won't tempt anyone to steal from my car." But, of course, I didn't listen to myself and I went upstairs. When I returned to my car, I noticed something different. My car window had been smashed and all of the luggage and retail clothing had been stolen. In that moment, I didn't panic. I thought to myself, well that's my karma, and I told you so, so you now have to suffer the consequences of paying back all those vendors for the stolen clothing. Apparently, it was a lesson I had to learn.

In that moment, a young man came outside and asked me if my car had also been broken into. I replied yes and asked about the other "victims". He gave me a list of the things stolen. I told him that I own a yoga studio and that all of my yoga clothing had been taken with my luggage. His eyes widened and said "Yoga clothing?!" I said, yes. He asked me to follow him to the lobby office and I did. When I opened the door to the office, all of my clothing was laid out across the desks and chairs. Plus, my luggage was there too, which, if I may add, was from an expensive brand so it was valuable. Apparently, the robber couldn't carry the luggage because it was too heavy so he put it behind a wall to come back and get later. The superintendent of the building saw it and brought it into the lobby since it looked suspicious.

So, if we break down the story, I will explain the different segments as they pertain to karma. My accumulated karma meant that this incident of getting my car broken into and getting my retail clothing stolen was going to happen to me some way or another. When the incident was happening I was burning karma in that moment. How I chose to react to the incident was what would either create more karma (positive or negative) or completely extinguish it (neutral.) When the incident happened, I had two choices, I could react and freak out, or I could have understood it as I did. I felt that since I was able to observe this incident as my responsibility, I was also able to reap the benefits of getting the belongings returned to me, which I understand as my karma as well. How I reacted in the moment of receiving the belongings again would also have its effect of either creating more karma or extinguishing it. Please do the exercise below to help you figure out how karma works in your daily life.

Step 13 Exercises

Karma Exercise

List one incident that happened to you recently.

One Incident:

_____
_____

   Discover how this incident may have come from your
accumulated karma. It could be something directly correlated
or it could be something from a previous lifetime. See if there
are any recent correlations from you previous actions that may
have triggered this incident to come up in order to experience
a lesson.

Accumulated Karma related to Incident:

_____
_____
_____

The moment you had the incident happen to you, you were
burning karma. Remember that moment. How were you
feeling?

_____
_____
_____
_____

How did you react to the incident?

_____
_____
_____

Did you feel like a victim? Why or why not?

_____

_____

_____

How do you feel you might have created karma from that
reaction? Was it positive? Negative? Or Neutral?

_____

_____

_____

_____

What action could you take next time that could cause a
different karmic effect?

_____

_____

_____

_____

Personal Exercises

Define what taking something personal means:

_____

_____

_____

Recall a moment when you took something personal:

_____

_____

_____

Why did you take it personally?

_____

_____

_____

Was the person hurting you intentionally?

_____

_____

_____

If so, why do you think they wanted to hurt you?
What were they feeling?

_____

_____

_____

If the person was not hurting you intentionally, why do you
feel the need to take it personally?

_____

_____

_____

Is it your ego or your Pure Self that wants to take it
personally?

_____

Why?

_____

_____

_____

   The exercises from the "What is Truth?" chapter are helpful
for this step as well. But, most importantly, you want to discover
that others' actions are completely independent of you.

Your thoughts on discovering everyone else is reacting based
on his/her belief system(s) and relative truth:

_____

_____

_____

_____

_____

Step 14

Forgive Others

*"Let us forgive each other –
only then will we live in peace."*

– Leo Nikolaevich Tolstoy

Everyone else's story is just like yours in that it is relative. Therefore, you know that they are suffering just like you are. Since you have already discovered that everyone else also has their own belief systems that drive him or her to act the way they do, it's only natural to start to find some compassion and acceptance for them. If you are reading this step and saying to yourself, "No way, they did this to me," then I would argue that you probably haven't forgiven yourself or found compassion for yourself yet. The moment you can truly find that, it will be a lot easier to discover this step. These last few steps are the most difficult to attain. You must discover them and experience them for yourself first.

Most importantly, in this step, it would be beneficial for you to forgive those persons that you feel have enforced this chosen belief system for your behavior. If you understand that they were acting out of their relative truth and belief system unconsciously, then the process has begun. If they had been conscious of the effects that their behaviors and actions had on you, they may have thought twice about what they did. Either way, it is never personal so it is ok.

Another factor to take into consideration is that you are on a healing path and are looking to better your life. Not everyone is on this path, nor do they even know it exists. Therefore, they may be stuck incessantly in suffering if they don't choose to find a way to heal. They may spend their whole life in delusion, living in ignorance, and sleepwalking though life. Hopefully that causes a bit of sorrow in your heart, which can be translated as compassion. If you truly do put yourself in others' shoes, you will see how they are stuck in a cycle of pain, just as you have been.

You most likely were looking for love and acceptance for being yourself and who you truly are, just like me and the people in my case studies. You didn't want to have to change yourself in order to have others love you or accept you. But you probably couldn't find that love and acceptance, and you felt rejected and alone. So, this is where your belief system started kicking in. You asked yourself, "What do I do in order to fit into this world? I can change myself, my natural self, and start adapting to my surroundings." I promise you that if you did this unconsciously, then 99.9% of everyone you have interacted with in your entire life, including your parents, grandparents, kids, friends, etc., has also done this.

Anytime someone, like yourself, comes into more awareness, it is inevitable that he/she questions his/her life and actions. Be grateful that the universe allowed you to begin to come to this realization and choose to heal in this moment. Find some peace and love in your heart for all of those other suffering beings who have not been blessed to find some peace and don't even know where to start. Remember when you were in that position and find some compassion and acceptance for those who don't have what you do.

Step 14 Exercises

Forgiveness Exercise

Take a moment to write down two main characters in your life that you feel have hurt you or caused you to suffer. You can do this below or in your journal if you need more space. Start with two and feel free to go through more if you need to.

Person 1:

_____

Person 2:

_____

Answer the following questions for each character individually and patiently. Take your time.

Person's Name:

_____

Person's Relationship to you:

_____

At what age did this person begin their relationship to you (i.e., mother could be at birth, friend could be at age 10, etc.):

_____

Are you still actively in a relationship with this person? (Do you see this person often or have conversations with them?):

_____

Why or why not?:

_____

Is this someone you wish you could forgive?

_____

What was the action that this person did towards you that you find unforgivable?

_____

_____

_____

_____

Did this person act from a place of ego or pure self when they behaved in this way? (refer to "What is Truth?" chapter.)

_____

_____

Did you react to this person's actions or behavior from a place of ego or pure self?

_____

_____

_____

_____

Are you hearing a justification in your mind for your actions?

_____

_____

Was this person possibly reacting unconsciously, using his/her belief system(s) to defend him/herself against you or someone else?

_____

_____

_____

_____

Does this person have their own relative truth about what happened and their side of the story?

_____

_____

_____

Does this person suffer and feel pain just like you?

_____

_____

Do you want to feel liberated from this person's power and control over your emotions and feelings in order to find inner peace?

_____

_____

_____

_____

Then forgive them consciously and compassionately. Use an affirmation if it helps and let them go!

Your thoughts on compassion for and forgiveness of others are

_____

_____

_____

_____

_____

_____

Step 15

Practicing the Process

"Never be in a hurry; do everything quietly and in a calm spirit. Do not lose your inner peace for anything whatsoever, even if your whole world seems upset."

- St. Francis de Sales

Now, let's piece this all together and put it into action. When confronted with a situation that stirs up old thoughts and behavioral patterns, stop and remind yourself of the relative truth behind the belief system that has triggered your reactions before. Overcome your relative truth by changing your thoughts and actions in that moment in order to be in harmony with how you truly feel. I know that this might all be conceptual right now, but I promise you that the process starts with concepts that you feel are beneficial for you and that you want to adapt to your life. Eventually, the concepts become reality, slowly and with patience. This is a new affirmation to adopt, so to speak.

A good question to ask yourself in the moment of truth is, "What will maintain my peace?" By asking yourself this question, you will need to check in with your deeper true self for the answer in that exact moment and act consciously from there.

Another way of putting this into practice is to catch yourself in the moment that a habitual thought or behavior appears. If you have trouble with this, it may be helpful to have a reminder like a bracelet, string, or index card that is meant to be a warning flag for you. This way, when a situation arises that might trigger your unconscious thoughts and behaviors, you can catch yourself in the act. Stop, observe, become aware, and then act consciously. Use a positive affirmation and make the necessary changes to your behavior so that you have a favorable outcome.

Check in with your feelings in that moment. When you feel something but you act differently or say something different from how you feel, you begin to chip away at yourself again. You already know that this behavior is harmful, so shift it on the spot. Hear your unconscious negative affirmation and in that moment, mentally repeat the conscious positive affirmation over and over again.

I have tried to give you experiential exercises in this book in order to help you gain some wisdom about yourself. To read a book is to attain more knowledge, but books don't provide as much benefit if you can't apply what you are learning in your brain to practical day-to-day scenarios. Experience implies gaining wisdom, so hopefully you can at least shift yourself once a week and act consciously instead of reacting habitually and unconsciously. I can assure you that by applying these steps you will begin to develop greater inner peace.

The power to create new experiences will change your life. Living consciously and presently is what will make this life beautiful and vivid. First, you'll need to start to heal the things that bring you down and weigh heavily on you. You were given a blessed life by being a human being with free will and the possibility of spiritual growth. You are a sentient being that can choose to be conscious. You may say that you are already conscious and you are probably right, but how much of your day is spent in this consciousness?

If consciousness and awareness of your true self lead to peace and happiness, then wouldn't you want to be conscious the majority of the time? The moment you catch yourself being reactive or wrapped up in your story, stop and take a deep breath. Ask yourself, "What is the relative truth behind this situation? And what is the absolute truth? What is the unconscious affirmation in my mind right now? How do I feel right now and how can I act accordingly? What will maintain my peace?"

You still need to live in this worldly life and pay the bills. You can do that with every moment being painful. Or you can do it peacefully, accepting that this is the reality you and the universe have chosen for you and that it's what you have to live right now. It's not forever, just right now. Don't let the past and future weigh heavily on you. As you start to heal, you will feel lighter. It's a sure sign that you are heading in a peaceful direction.

Cheat Sheet of the Steps

When you are confronted with a situation, thought, memory, feeling, or person that begins to stress you out or disturb your peace, use PARA-CHOOSE! Pause, Ask, Repeat, Ask, and CHOOSE!

1. Pause.

2. Ask yourself, "Who is talking?" Ego or pure self? If the answer is pure self, then listen. If the answer is the ego,

3. Repeat your conscious affirmation at least seven times in your head.

4. Ask yourself, "What action will maintain my peace?"

5. CHOOSE the appropriate conscious action based on your thoughts and emotions connected to your pure self.

Remember that not taking an action is also an action. Also, use this formula to analyze the circumstances of a situation that you have already reacted to. Think about how you can maintain your peace better the next time you are confronted with a similar situation. And, believe me, you will have plenty of opportunities to practice maintaining your peace. Find some gratitude for those moments because they provide the lessons we must learn and without those disturbed moments, we wouldn't be able to find the peaceful ones. "Thank your for being my teacher" is an affirmation I use constantly when I am confronted with the hardest of lessons, either by people or circumstances. This affirmation provides gratitude and humility all at the same time—two of the most important lessons to learn.

Step 15 Exercises

What Action Will Maintain my Peace? Exercise

This exercise is similar to the Maintaining Inner Peace exercise from Step 1: Have Inner Peace? But, this time I want you to think of three decisions you made since you started reading this book that have stayed with you as things that you wish you had done differently in order to have seen and felt better results. Make these decisions relevant to your behavior if possible. Every action you make is a decision, so choose the three that resonate with you the most.

Decision 1:

_____

_____

_____

Decision 2:

_____

_____

_____

Decision 3:

_____

_____

_____

Now, choose three other decisions that you made since you started reading this book, but let these decisions be examples of how you paused before reacting and had a different outcome than usual. This is a bit confusing to me. Not exactly sure what you mean here.   Close your eyes and take your time. They might not jump out at you at first and they may even seem small and insignificant, but I guarantee you that these three examples are the first step to consciously choosing your inner peace. If you can't think of any decisions off hand, just think of three things that you decided today or this past week that maintained your peace. Maybe it's just as easy as your deciding to continue reading this book in order to heal from within.

Decision 1:

_____

_____

_____

Decision 2:

_____

_____

_____

Decision 3:

_____

_____

_____

Inner Peace Definition Exercise

After reading this book and going through your process so far, has your definition of inner peace changed? If so, please redefine inner peace below.

_____

_____

_____

_____

_____

Appendixes

APPENDIX A
How to Use the 15-Step Table

On page 180 there is a table that briefly identifies the steps. Please make a few photocopies of this table for your own personal use, as you may need to use it for different behaviors and patterns. There is a blank column so that you can write your conclusions. Use a journal or spare sheet of paper for brainstorming and working on the exercises after each step. Use the table once you have concluded what your answers might be. Be concise and specific. If you tend to like to write it all out like I do, then use your journal. Once you are done writing it all out, place your more specific, concise answers in the table. This will keep the steps clear and simple in your mind. We are looking for clarity, not clutter.

Remember, you are starting to dig up dirt, so you will uncover all sorts of unknown things, treasures and mud alike. You might realize or discover something very beautiful about yourself – your thoughts and behaviors don't always have to be negative. Do the steps for a positive behavior as well.

When you get to "What is Truth?", "Forgive Yourself", "Nothing is Personal" and "Forgive Others", write your thoughts about the topics. It might be helpful to write down that you are in the process of realizing these steps, as that can serve as a conscious positive affirmation as well. You could expand on your thoughts only if you feel you want to in your journal.

For "Practicing the Process", write one example from

within the week or month you started the process of a time when you were able to apply some of these steps, act consciously, and begin to break your pattern. Write down how applying the steps made you feel.

Remember, there are no right or wrong answers. There are only your answers in this moment.

15-Step Table

STEP 1: Have Inner Peace?	
STEP 2: Choose a Behavior, any Behavior	
STEP 3: Charge of Behavior	
STEP 4: Penny for Your Thoughts	
STEP 5: Charge of Thoughts	
STEP 6: Broken Record in Your Mind	
STEP 7: Whose Thoughts are These?	
STEP 8: Effect of Thoughts	
STEP 9: It's a Vicious Cycle	
STEP 10: What is Truth?	
STEP 11: Change Your Mind	
STEP 12: Forgive Yourself	
STEP 13: Nothing is Personal	
STEP 14: Forgive Others	
STEP 15: Practicing the Process	

APPENDIX B

15-Step Table, Example 1

STEP 1: Have Inner Peace?	Most of the time.
STEP 2: Choose a Behavior, any Behavior	Have trouble saying, "No."
STEP 3: Charge of Behavior	Positive and negative. Makes me feel good to help, but it eventually takes away sense of self and healthy boundaries.
STEP 4: Penny for Your Thoughts	The person needs help. I have the means and ability to help them. I feel guilty if I don't. I become a people pleaser.
STEP 5: Charge of Thoughts	Positive and negative. Same as #3.
STEP 6: Broken Record in Your Mind	"I won't be loved if I don't say yes."
STEP 7: Whose Thoughts are These?	Family – childhood conditioning. I had to say yes for harmony in the family. If not I would suffer the consequences.
STEP 8: Effect of Thoughts	Harmful. The thoughts erode my sense of self... genuine authenticity by not having proper boundaries.
STEP 9: It's a Vicious Cycle	I need to say yes or face the consequences of not being loved or accepted. Fear of rejection.
STEP 10: What is Truth?	It may have served in childhood but it no longer does as an adult.
STEP 11: Change Your Mind	"I am loved as I am. My feelings, thoughts, and words all agree."
STEP 12: Forgive Yourself	I can forgive myself. I would never want to hurt myself or take away from my authenticity.

STEP 13: Nothing is Personal	Everyone else is a result of their own previous experiences. They are a product of their own environment as they grew up.
STEP 14: Forgive Others	I have forgiven all who have harmed me – intentionally and unintentionally.
STEP 15: Practicing the Process	I was asked for a monetary favor. I said no. Instead I helped the person figure out a solution. It felt empowering.

15-Step Table, Example 2

STEP 1: Have Inner Peace?	Mostly, yet I find I feel like I am often going through the motions of life without truly pushing myself.
STEP 2: Choose a Behavior, any Behavior	Initial inspiration, midterm complacency, long term boredom. Acceptance of feeling just "ok" with work.
STEP 3: Charge of Behavior	Negative
STEP 4: Penny for Your Thoughts	I am not good enough or putting enough thought or focus behind my actions to be considered successful. Anxiety about needing to perform or being evaluated.
STEP 5: Charge of Thoughts	Negative
STEP 6: Broken Record in Your Mind	"I am les than worthy. I don't deserve this."
STEP 7: Whose Thoughts are These?	Family – five siblings who excelled. Parents – no pressure means having pressure. And people in my social group were all "successful."
STEP 8: Effect of Thoughts	Harmful in feeling like I had to be successful in many areas at a young age, beneficial in that I had great role models for striving for success and happiness.

STEP 9: It's a Vicious Cycle	If I face the world as "happy" I will be considered successful and make others feel good. Being the best means success, which means happiness.
STEP 10: What is Truth?	*
STEP 11: Change Your Mind	"I am worthy, deserving and focused."
STEP 12: Forgive Yourself	*
STEP 13: Nothing is Personal	*
STEP 14: Forgive Others	*
STEP 15: Practicing the Process	*

* These steps were not discussed or processed with the case study in my presence, which is why they are left in blank.

15-Step Table, Example 3

STEP 1: Have Inner Peace?	No.
STEP 2: Choose a Behavior, any Behavior	Shy and withdrawn from society.
STEP 3: Charge of Behavior	Negative.
STEP 4: Penny for Your Thoughts	Fear of being unloved, abandoned and rejected.
STEP 5: Charge of Thoughts	Negative.
STEP 6: Broken Record in Your Mind	I am not good enough.
STEP 7: Whose Thoughts are These?	My mother was withdrawn and didn't show emotions.
STEP 8: Effect of Thoughts	Harmful.

STEP 9: It's a Vicious Cycle	Because of my fear of rejection, I created a defense mechanism that "guarded" me from being hurt by others by withdrawing from them first.
STEP 10: What is Truth?	*
STEP 11: Change Your Mind	"I am loved and accepted for who I am."
STEP 12: Forgive Yourself	*
STEP 13: Nothing is Personal	*
STEP 14: Forgive Others	*
STEP 15: Practicing the Process	*

* These steps were not discussed or processed with the case study in my presence, which is why they are left in blank.

CASE STUDIES

Case Study 1: Dan, mid 50s

1. Have Peace?: When I asked Dan if he was at peace, he said, "No."

2. Choose a Behavior: He mentioned the action of "drinking too much."

3. Charge of Behavior: Then, he said that the behavior was both positive and negative; it was positive because it helped him interact with people better and be accepted, but negative because now he can't sleep because of the alcohol. It is now hurting him more than helping him.

4. Penny for Your Thoughts: Dan told me about were that he drank to relax. Relaxing is the desired result and not a thought, but a desire. He always felt awkward in social settings, so he started drinking so that he would appeal to people and fit in more easily. I dug deeper to find the initial thoughts right before he took a sip of alcohol and he said that it had more to do with "winding down and not knowing any other way of doing it." He found comfort in the drink even though he knew it was hurtful.

5. Charge of Thoughts: He concluded that his thoughts were more negative than positive.

6. Broken Record in Your Mind: His unconscious affirmation was that he was awkward and uncomfortable in social gatherings. So he repeated to himself, "I am awkward and uncomfortable."

7. Source of Thoughts: He initially stated his feelings

of social discomfort started when he was 17 years old. He would be with a group and feel uncomfortable and socially awkward, and so he started drinking to feel better and fit in. In other words, he felt he couldn't be himself because no one liked him that way. So, he concluded that these thoughts came from society, meaning society taught him that in order to fit in, he had to drink. Once we searched a little deeper, he discovered that before alcohol, he smoked cigarettes, and before cigarettes, he turned to eating excessively. So, when we went backwards in time, he said he always felt awkward as a child and that he was ridiculed and made fun of, so he felt he had to change himself in order to better fit in with society and his family.

8. Effect of Thoughts: He concluded that his thoughts were harmful.

9. It's a Vicious Cycle: Here he had to allow me to help him find some uncovered belief system. I reflected his words back to him when he said felt he had to change himself in order to be accepted, and started to ask him some deeper questions. It resulted in him saying that he had a fear of rejection and of getting his feelings hurt, so he modified himself in order to fit into society. His belief system was that if he wanted to be liked and feel comfortable in his own skin, he had to change who he naturally was and do things that were socially acceptable, even if it was detrimental to him. So, he lived many years with this belief system that only festered deeper and deeper into his thoughts, which, in turn, affected his life. But, now he has had it and wants to find a way to heal himself.

10. What is Truth?: If Dan can realize that he needed that behavioral pattern at a certain time in his life but not anymore, then he can start to heal. He doesn't need that behavior anymore.

11. Change your Mind: He changed his unconscious affirmation to a conscious one: "I am relaxed and focused."

12. Forgive Yourself: He forgave himself for all the actions he did in the past that perpetuated this behavior and made him more lost. Without the addictive behavior of drinking alcohol, he wouldn't be here now. He realized that it was part of his story.

13. Nothing is Personal: Dan realized that society and his friends and family all have their own separate belief systems that unconsciously motivate them to act in ways to protect themselves too. So, maybe the guy that pushed him to drink the most also feared rejection and felt that if he didn't find another person to drink with, he would feel awkward as well. Who knows what each person's story is, but if you can at least realize that everyone does have one, then you can heal more.

14. Forgive Others: It will be important for Dan to forgive those people who directly influenced his life to instill this behavior pattern. Since he realized the above, it is easier for him to find compassion for them, because they too are looking for some love and acceptance.

15. Put it into Practice: Every time Dan is confronted with the possibility of having a drink, he has to review these steps and observe what he should do in that moment for the sake of his peace. He has to repeat his conscious affirmation in order to start to change himself. He has to ask himself, "What will maintain or bring me inner peace?" And he will know what to do. He will also have moments when he can choose to either act a certain way in order to blend in with society so that he is accepted or consciously act according to how he truly feels inside, for himself, without the fear of rejection. His gut will know what to do, and hopefully he will act harmoniously, but he must remind himself of this process in order to create awareness.

Case Study 2: Patricia, mid 30s

1. Have Peace?: Before coming to any conclusions, Patricia and I started our session with the meditation exercise, which included writing her thoughts. When she finished and I asked her to find a common theme, she became emotional. She shared that she suffers from depression. So, our answer to the question if she has inner peace is "No."

2. Choose a Behavior: After speaking for a little bit, we identified the following behavior pattern: "I don't allow anyone to help me. I do things on my own."

3. Charge of Behavior: She expressed that this behavior was negative.

4. Penny for Your Thoughts: She mentioned that when approached by someone who wants to help her she says in her mind, "No, it's ok. I can handle this on my own. I got it." When we went a step deeper, she found that she feared rejection and not being accepted as she truly naturally is, which is an emotional woman with positive and negative emotions alike. So, she took care of everything and pretended everything was ok on the outside. She didn't allow anyone to be close to her life so that they wouldn't discover the truth about her.

5. Charge of Thoughts: She identified this behavior of not allowing others to help her and have complete control as being negative.

6. Broken Record in Your Mind: The unconscious negative affirmation she repeated to herself was, "I have to be perfect or else I won't be loved."

7. Source of Thoughts: Patricia shared that she felt this behavior came from her parents and her childhood. Her parents didn't like her to express any negative emotions. She was forced to hide those emotions and to not have them at all. Negative emotions meant she was bad. So, therefore, she had to be perfect and good and only show her positive emotions, even if they were false. If she was taught to repress her negative emotions at an early age, this of course, may be why she suffers from depression. Her whole body is dying to express itself in a healthy way and get all that negativity out. With all that negativity inside her body, she will continue to be depressed.

8. Effect of Thoughts: She concluded that these thoughts were harmful to her.

9. It's a Vicious Cycle: Her belief system was that the way to cope and survive in her situation was to close herself off from everyone around. She believed that needing help implied a weakness and a negative emotion, therefore, this person had to isolate herself and believe that she could do everything on her own, especially because if someone did help her, they might find out she has negative emotions and that are "wrong." So, she created a wall around her, protecting herself from the world that was not accepting of her true, natural feelings. She had to be perfect in school, at home, with her family, with her friends, in her career, etc. But, of course, being perfect in that way is impossible. Most children are taught that the idea of being successful in every aspect in your life is the way to be perfect, but that is not true.

10. What is Truth?: She realized that this behavior was required of her at a young age in order for her to survive. It might have worked to a small degree back then, and it's what she needed to do to protect herself. But now, she can see the relative truth of the situation and she realizes that does not have to be her truth any longer. She was of course more unconscious back then and reacting to her surroundings in the best way she knew how.

11. Change your Mind: The conscious positive affirmation was, "I am loved. I accept myself the way that I am right now."

12. Forgive Yourself: Forgiving herself for all the past actions that might have instilled and further created this behavioral pattern is going to help her heal. Not placing blame on herself but accepting her life as her responsibility will be imperative for her healing process.

13. Nothing is Personal: She understood that her parents did the best they could and were also raised to hide their negative feelings, so they taught that to her unconsciously.

14. Forgive Others: She forgave her parents for their actions and did not place blame on them. She found compassion for her parents, because they too had suffered just like she did as a child. All they wanted to do was cry or express pain, but they were conditioned not to. As a more conscious being than before, can you possibly place blame on someone when you know they acted out of fear and pain and suffering as well, even if they weren't aware of it?

15. Put it into Practice: Every time Patricia is confronted with a situation where someone wants to help her, she needs to stop and remind herself what she discovered from these steps. She will need to repeat her conscious affirmation whenever it is needed until it becomes her new thought pattern. She will make the decision based on the answer to, "What will maintain or bring me inner peace?"

She will also confront situations when she will habitually want to hide how she truly feels or act as if everything is fine, but she will need to remind herself of this process and note that she has to act consciously in order to benefit herself. Instead of choosing the habitual behavior, she has to take a step back, stop, observe and act in accordance with how she feels without fear of rejection, since that fear doesn't have to control her life anymore. She can create a new affirmation that is healthy and consists of the following thoughts: "I feel something, and it's ok to express and verbalize it in the way that it needs to come out naturally and organically." In Patricia's case, she will need to figure out how to constructively express all of these bottled up negative emotions. Maybe doing the 15 steps for each emotion might be beneficial.

APPENDIX C
Recommended Readings

The Yoga Sutras of Patanjali
translated by Swami Satchidadanda

The Autobiography of a Yogi
by Paramahansa Yogananda

A New Earth
by Eckhart Tolle

The Way of the Peaceful Warrior
by Dan Millman

Anatomy of the Spirit
by Caroline Myss

You Can Heal Your Life
by Louise Hay

Celestine Prophecy
by James Redfield

A Separate Reality
by Carlos Castaneda

The Tao of Pooh
by Benjamin Hoff

Siddhartha
by Hermann Hesse

Gates to Buddhist Practice:
Essential Teachings from a Tibetan Master
by Tulku Chagdud

The Words of My Perfect Teacher
by Patrul Rinpoche

The Quickening
by Stuart Wilde

Just Be Publications

www.rinayoga.com